THE
5-MINUTE

PRAYER
PLAN

FOR DADS

© 2022 by Barbour Publishing, Inc.

Print ISBN 978-1-63609-165-5

Some text previously published in *The 5-Minute Prayer Plan for Men*, published by Barbour Publishing.

Published by Barbour Publishing, Inc., 1810 Barbour Drive, Uhrichsville, Ohio 44683, www.barbourbooks.com

Our mission is to inspire the world with the life-changing message of the Bible.

Member of the
Evangelical Christian
Publishers Association

Printed in the United States of America.

A GUIDE TO MORE FOCUSED PRAYER

THE
5-MINUTE

PRAYER
PLAN

FOR DADS

ED CYZEWSKI

BARBOUR
PUBLISHING

INTRODUCTION

Fatherhood demands sacrifice, attention, and compassion. Your children require a drastic change in priorities and dramatically alter how you spend your time. The joy and love they bring makes that shift well worthwhile, yet throughout the highs and lows of parenthood, prayer can fall by the wayside. At a time when you need to be especially aware of the parental love that God has for you, those quiet moments of devotion can get squeezed out of your day. With all the uncertainty and disruption that comes from children, dads need a simple path toward intimacy with God the Father, Son, and Holy Spirit.

This practical and inspirational book will open up new ways into prayer with 90+ "5-Minute" plans for your daily quiet time. You'll explore reading plans that touch on prayer's intersection with common parenting themes including compassion, obedience, repentance, and forgiveness, as well as more general topics such as intercession, wealth, mercy, repentance, witnessing, worry, gratitude, protection, work, relationships, church, government, and the future. A handy subject index in the back of the book will help you find these topics quickly.

Each entry includes:

- Minute 1: A scripture to meditate on

- Minutes 2–3: Specific prayer points and questions to consider as you enter a time of prayer

- Minutes 4–5: A jump-starter prayer to springboard you into a time of conversation with God

The prayers in this book have been written with you in mind, each word penned in prayer, asking the Lord to give insight into the needs of those who will pick this book up and begin a new or renewed journey with Him. God, our Father in heaven, is compassionate, merciful, and, most importantly, present in those quiet moments when you stand transparently before the One with arms wide open to embrace you in unconditional love.

GOD'S PEOPLE WAIT
FOR GOD ALONE

*For God alone my soul waits in silence; from him comes
my salvation. He alone is my rock and my salvation,
my fortress; I shall never be shaken. How long will you
assail a person, will you batter your victim, all of you,
as you would a leaning wall, a tottering fence? Their
only plan is to bring down a person of prominence. They
take pleasure in falsehood; they bless with their mouths,
but inwardly they curse. For God alone my soul waits
in silence, for my hope is from him. He alone is my rock
and my salvation, my fortress; I shall not be shaken. On
God rests my deliverance and my honor; my mighty rock,
my refuge is in God. Trust in him at all times, O people;
pour out your heart before him; God is a refuge for us.*

PSALM 62:1–8 NRSV

- What are you waiting for God to do right now? How
  has this time of waiting tested your faith in God?

- Is there something that you need to surrender to
  God or that you need to wait for in silence? Is this
  time of waiting a source of fear or anxiety?

- God's reliability and trustworthiness are contrasted
  with those who are scheming and duplicitous. How
  has God's reliability come up in your life?

- This psalm notes waiting for "God alone," but are
  there times when we end up waiting for something
  or someone else to help or provide for us?

- What would it look like for God to become your fortress and rock in this season of life?

- Is there something in your life that has shaken you or prompted you to go to God in prayer? What has that experience revealed about where you place your faith?

- How does trusting in God alone impact your reputation and honor? Is there a fear that God won't intervene or that God won't meet your expectations?

Jesus, I surrender my uncertainty, my fears, and my struggles to Your care, and I ask for Your grace to wait in patience for Your help and deliverance for the challenges of today and in the future. May my faith in Your loving care grow as I learn to depend on You as my rock and my fortress of protection. Teach me to value the transformative moments of silent waiting on You, as every other form of protection and deliverance melts away and Your presence alone remains. Amen.

PRAYER IS ROOTED IN GOD'S LOVE

As for other matters, brothers and sisters, pray for us that the message of the Lord may spread rapidly and be honored, just as it was with you. And pray that we may be delivered from wicked and evil people, for not everyone has faith. But the Lord is faithful, and he will strengthen you and protect you from the evil one. We have confidence in the Lord that you are doing and will continue to do the things we command. May the Lord direct your hearts into God's love and Christ's perseverance. . . . Now may the Lord of peace himself give you peace at all times and in every way. The Lord be with all of you.

2 Thessalonians 3:1–5, 16 NIV

- Paul wrote to a church experiencing conflict and division, but he saw that the Lord would remain faithful to deliver and strengthen His people. Is there a challenge or a conflict that you're facing today and you need to call on God's intervention?

- While facing the challenges of life, Paul remained focused on praying that the Lord's message would continue to spread. How would this particular focus impact the way you approach each day?

- Do you tend to believe that God will faithfully deliver you, or do you sometimes worry that you're left on your own? How can you turn to God in the midst of these challenges?

- Paul specifically prayed that the Thessalonians' hearts would be directed by the Lord to God's love and Christ's perseverance. How can the assurance of God's love help you face the challenges and doubts of your prayer life?

- Are there particular values, goals, or people that have impacted the direction of your life each day?

- While circumstances may remain turbulent or uncertain, it is appropriate to ask God for the peace that comes with His presence. How can you make space today for God's presence and peace?

- Where do most people seek peace today? How does the peace of this world compare to the peace that God gives?

Jesus, You have come into our world to unite me with the love of the Father, and I benefit from the peace that comes from God's generous presence. Help me to leave behind my sources of comfort and my plans for peace that keep me from entering into Your rest. Help me to make space today for Your message and to live in obedience to Your commands. Direct me deeper into Your love and presence today. Amen.

SPIRITUAL DEAD ENDS

"Is anyone thirsty? Come and drink—even if you have no money! Come, take your choice of wine or milk—it's all free! Why spend your money on food that does not give you strength? Why pay for food that does you no good? Listen to me, and you will eat what is good. You will enjoy the finest food. . . . Seek the LORD while you can find him. Call on him now while he is near. Let the wicked change their ways and banish the very thought of doing wrong. Let them turn to the LORD that he may have mercy on them. Yes, turn to our God, for he will forgive generously. "My thoughts are nothing like your thoughts," says the LORD. "And my ways are far beyond anything you could imagine. For just as the heavens are higher than the earth, so my ways are higher than your ways and my thoughts higher than your thoughts."

ISAIAH 55:1-2, 6-9 NLT

- What are you listening to today? Consider the voices that are impacting you and directing you and whether they are satisfying your deeper needs.

- Why do people pursue things that fail to satisfy them or nourish them? Do you approach God believing in promises like today's passage about God offering to satisfy His people?

- What are the reasons it's difficult at times to trust God's promises about satisfying you?

- Today is the day to receive God's forgiveness and mercy, but what do you expect will happen if you turn to God and ask for forgiveness?

- Isaiah told the people of Israel to call on God while He was near to them. Why do God's people sometimes hesitate to call out for God? Are there ways you relate to this?

- As you enter into prayer today, consider that God's thoughts and ways are higher than your own. How does this promise impact the way you express yourself and make requests to God?

Lord, You have assured me that Your wisdom far exceeds my own and that You are extending mercy and grace to me today, promising forgiveness and satisfaction. Open my eyes to the wonders of Your presence and wisdom, and help me to move beyond the distractions of my life that crowd out the redemptive work You long to do. May I turn to You whenever I have done wrong and extend Your mercy and forgiveness to others just as I have received it. Amen.

STEPS FOR
GAINING WISDOM

The days of our life are seventy years, or perhaps eighty, if we are strong; even then their span is only toil and trouble; they are soon gone, and we fly away. Who considers the power of your anger? Your wrath is as great as the fear that is due you. So teach us to count our days that we may gain a wise heart. Turn, O LORD! How long? Have compassion on your servants! Satisfy us in the morning with your steadfast love, so that we may rejoice and be glad all our days. Make us glad as many days as you have afflicted us, and as many years as we have seen evil. Let your work be manifest to your servants, and your glorious power to their children. Let the favor of the Lord our God be upon us, and prosper for us the work of our hands—O prosper the work of our hands!

PSALM 90:10-17 NRSV

- The psalms frequently mention seeking God in the morning. Is there a reason this often comes up as a spiritual practice? When are you most receptive to the voice of God?

- There is no avoiding the fleeting nature of life and the hard work that consumes many days on earth. How can you gain wisdom by meditating on the brief nature of life on earth? How does this allow you to focus on what is most important?

- While calling out for God's favor and compassion, the psalmist is also very aware of God's wrath. How have you maintained a healthy perspective on each?

- When have you lost sight of God's compassion and mercy? How did this impact the way you prayed?

- Although there is a lot of work to be done on earth, God doesn't desire for His people to be miserable or to feel trapped. How can you offer your work to God today?

- What does it look like to experience God's favor on the work of your hands? Are there ways you can invite God to be present in your work each day?

Father, You offer me wisdom and knowledge by revealing the fleeting nature of life on earth. May I count the number of my days and take note of the consequences of disobedience so that I make wise choices and trust You to guide me into obedience. May Your compassion meet me in my time of need, and may I enjoy Your restoration today. Amen.

TRUST GOD IN DISAPPOINTING TIMES

*This is what the L**ORD** says: "You will be in Babylon for
seventy years. But then I will come and do for you all
the good things I have promised, and I will bring you
home again. For I know the plans I have for you," says
the L**ORD**. "They are plans for good and not for disaster,
to give you a future and a hope. In those days when
you pray, I will listen. If you look for me wholeheartedly,
you will find me. I will be found by you," says the L**ORD**.
"I will end your captivity and restore your fortunes.
I will gather you out of the nations where I sent you
and will bring you home again to your own land."*

JEREMIAH 29:10–14 NLT

♦ The people of Israel wanted to be restored to their
land, and they even had prophets telling them that
it would come to pass soon. However, the Lord said
they would be exiled for seventy years, a reality that
God's people struggled with. How can you relate to
this tendency to seek alternatives to a difficult truth?

♦ God promised to bless and prosper His people even
in the extremely challenging circumstances of exile
in a foreign country. Are you facing a difficult season
or have you emerged from one? What does it mean
to you that God promises to bring blessings during
a hard time?

♦ After long stretches of disobedience and unfaithfulness that brought judgment and punishment, the

people of Israel were offered renewal and a new hope with God. What does this kind of restoration and blessing look like for you?

- ◆ Do you fear that God can't forgive you or restore you? How does this story impact your desire to pray?

- ◆ God can bring His people out of extremely hazardous circumstances and restore them to prosperity. Are there situations in your life that feel particularly hopeless right now? How can you offer them to God?

Lord, You restored the people of Israel while they were in exile. Even after they disobeyed Your commands and rejected You for generations, even after their unfaithfulness, You promised to bless them and to lead them into freedom once again. Help me to see the things that keep me from You, and lead me away from reliance on my own plans and resources. May I receive the complete healing You promise and enter the rest You offer. Amen.

THE CERTAIN PATH
TO A GOOD LIFE

Children, obey your parents in the Lord, for this is right. "Honor your father and mother"—this is the first commandment with a promise: "so that it may be well with you and you may live long on the earth." And, fathers, do not provoke your children to anger, but bring them up in the discipline and instruction of the Lord.

EPHESIANS 6:1-4 NRSV

- Paul writes about God's new covenant, but the wisdom of the Ten Commandments remains a priority in this letter. Why would he take time to emphasize this point about children remaining obedient to their parents?

- What made this particular commandment stand out to Paul? Why do you think there's a promise attached to this commandment?

- How does this promise of life going well with you and living a long life on earth relate to obeying your parents? What kinds of advantages can you expect to gain if you take this commandment seriously?

- What does it look like for children to "honor" their father and mother? Why is it so important that God would command it in the first place?

- How can you teach your children to be obedient and to live by this commandment?

- In what ways could you undermine this commandment by provoking your children to anger? How can you prevent this from happening in your own family?

- The alternative to needless provocation is bringing your children up in the discipline and instruction of the Lord. What kinds of disciplines have you learned that you can pass on to your children?

- Take a moment to examine your life and consider whether you need to add a particular discipline or learn something you can pass on to your children. How can you grow in this area?

- What is one thing you can teach your children this week? How can raising your children in the "instruction of the Lord" become a regular practice for your family that helps build up the faith of your children?

Father, thank You for modeling patience, care, and blessings for me so that I can teach my children to grow in their understanding of You and in obedience to what You teach. May I encourage and help my children to be obedient and reverent toward You so that they can enjoy the benefits of Your loving presence. As You have shown patience to me and instructed me in the right way to go, help me to guide the paths of my children so that they enjoy the blessings of intimacy and security in You. Amen.

ASKING GOD FOR BOLDNESS

When they heard the report, all the believers lifted their voices together in prayer to God: "O Sovereign Lord, Creator of heaven and earth, the sea, and everything in them—you spoke long ago by the Holy Spirit through our ancestor David, your servant, saying, 'Why were the nations so angry? Why did they waste their time with futile plans? The kings of the earth prepared for battle; the rulers gathered together against the LORD and against his Messiah.' . . . And now, O Lord, hear their threats, and give us, your servants, great boldness in preaching your word. Stretch out your hand with healing power; may miraculous signs and wonders be done through the name of your holy servant Jesus." After this prayer, the meeting place shook, and they were all filled with the Holy Spirit. Then they preached the word of God with boldness.

ACTS 4:24-26, 29-31 NLT

- Early Christians faced the threats of powerful religious and government leaders. Is there someone in authority that you fear and need to pray about today?

- This prayer didn't ask for an end to the persecution or for greater religious freedom. They asked for boldness to share the Gospel. Is there a difficult area in your life where you need to ask God for boldness or courage to step out in faith?

- Have you experienced the tension of ministering to glorify Jesus alone? Are there ways that ministry or sharing the Gospel can get tangled up in gaining personal acclaim?

• Have you asked God to help you meet the challenges of your life today? Do you expect God to act on your behalf in response to these requests?

• What would it look like to minister to others in boldness and confidence from the Holy Spirit?

• Even if the plans of earth's kings and rulers are dismissed as "futile" compared to the power of God, how do the issues of politics and intrigue become distractions or barriers to the Gospel today?

• Is it possible to prioritize prayer with fellow believers? Are there benefits that could come from praying with Christians and seeking the Spirit's strength together?

Jesus, You have overcome the world, and You promise to conquer every ruler and authority set up against You. May our faith in You grow stronger today as we trust You to enable us to speak up with boldness and grace. May we serve in the Holy Spirit's power and strength, sharing Your healing presence with others and winning You the glory and acclaim. Amen.

FINDING GOD IN NATURE

Lᴏʀᴅ, our Lord, how majestic is your name in all the earth! You have set your glory in the heavens. Through the praise of children and infants you have established a stronghold against your enemies, to silence the foe and the avenger. When I consider your heavens, the work of your fingers, the moon and the stars, which you have set in place, what is mankind that you are mindful of them, human beings that you care for them? You have made them a little lower than the angels and crowned them with glory and honor. You made them rulers over the works of your hands; you put everything under their feet.

Pꜱᴀʟᴍ 8:1–6 ɴɪᴠ

- Can you make time today to step outside for a moment of prayer and awareness of God? What does nature tell you about God?

- How does failing to see the majesty of God in the world impact your daily outlook and decisions?

- This psalm uses the dramatic language of comparing the praise of children to a stronghold. How does this relate to the idea of becoming like little children to enter God's kingdom?

- Another benefit of meditating on God's creation is a greater sense of humility. How does considering the grandeur of God's world impact you today?

- Meditating on nature also conveys the grace of God toward all people as the caretakers of His beloved creation. When can you take a moment to appreciate creation today?

- How does the honor of being a caretaker of creation impact how you see yourself in general?

- Are there ways you can make more space to enjoy creation on a daily basis?

- If meditation on creation can lead us to an affirmation of humanity's place as beloved caretakers, what are some of the results of neglecting this meditation? Are there ways that we can lose sight of God or our value before God when we overlook His creation?

Lord, You created the world out of Your infinite goodness and desired to share it with humanity, placing us in a partnership role as caretakers of Your world. May we turn away from the distractions we choose over You and from our own prideful creations that forfeit our place as caretakers of Your creation. Guide us into the space we need each day so that we can enjoy the world as You've created it, experience Your loving presence, and fully live into our calling as people crowned by You with glory and honor. Amen.

IMITATING GOD'S COMPASSION FOR HIS CHILDREN

As a father has compassion on his children, so the LORD has compassion on those who fear him; for he knows how we are formed, he remembers that we are dust. The life of mortals is like grass, they flourish like a flower of the field; the wind blows over it and it is gone, and its place remembers it no more. But from everlasting to everlasting the LORD's love is with those who fear him, and his righteousness with their children's children—with those who keep his covenant and remember to obey his precepts.

PSALM 103:13-18 NIV

- How do you feel about God seeing your weakness and knowing you intimately? Is that comforting and reassuring or alarming and disconcerting? How does that impact your interest in prayer?

- In what ways may your own earthly father/child relationships impact the way you pray?

- Consider how you view your own children with compassion. How does that affect the ways you imagine God viewing you?

- How does a father balance compassion with training his children in obedience and goodness? What does that mean for your relationship with God today?

- Considering that life is fleeting like grass in the field, how can the everlasting love of the Lord provide stability for you and for the future generations of your children?

- Remember the times when your own father failed to have compassion on you or you failed to have compassion on your children. How did those experiences shape you and what can they teach you about your faith today?

- What is your understanding of the fear of the Lord? In what ways does the writer of this psalm connect the idea of "fearing the Lord" with love and obedience?

- How can you treat your children with compassion and love while also helping them understand the "fear of the Lord" without alienating them from God?

Father in heaven, You have shown patience and compassion, blessing me with Your everlasting love and the promise of generations of blessing for our faithfulness. Help me to show You the respect, reverence, and honor that You rightly deserve and to conduct myself with obedient faith throughout today. May Your compassion and love shape my heart so that I can display that love and compassion with my children and teach them to revere You for all the days of their lives. May they experience Your compassion and blessings today. Amen.

PRAYER YIELDS TO WHAT GOD WILLS

They went to a place called Gethsemane; and he said to his disciples, "Sit here while I pray." He took with him Peter and James and John, and began to be distressed and agitated. And he said to them, "I am deeply grieved, even to death; remain here, and keep awake." And going a little farther, he threw himself on the ground and prayed that, if it were possible, the hour might pass from him. He said, "Abba, Father, for you all things are possible; remove this cup from me; yet, not what I want, but what you want." He came and found them sleeping; and he said to Peter, "Simon, are you asleep? Could you not keep awake one hour? Keep awake and pray that you may not come into the time of trial; the spirit indeed is willing, but the flesh is weak."

MARK 14:32–38 NRSV

- Jesus prayed in faith that all things are possible for God, and yet He never exploited God's power for His own sake. What does this mean for you as you approach God in prayer?

- Based on the example of Jesus, we can see that a prayer of faith does not have to be tied to a specific outcome. How does this prayer inform your own petitions and requests to God?

- Why do you think Jesus took only a few of His disciples to join Him in prayer during His moment of greatest need? Who are the people you can rely on when you need prayer and support?

- How have you responded to those who have failed to pray with you or support you in a time of need?

- Are there ways you become more present for those who are suffering or who need greater support?

- The disciples intended to stay awake and pray, but they failed to watch and pray with Jesus. Is there an area of your life where you have failed to live up to your best intentions? Can you offer that area of your life to God today in prayer?

Jesus, You have carried our sorrow and suffered for our sake, submitting to the will of the Father for our benefit. May we trust in Your strength to overcome our weaknesses and to fulfill our best intentions in prayer. Stay with us as we face suffering, send people of faith to hold us up when we are faltering, and help us to see the ways we can support those in need. Amen.

GOD IS PRESENT
AFTER A FAILURE

"I said, 'I have been banished from your sight;
yet I will look again toward your holy temple.'
The engulfing waters threatened me, the deep
surrounded me; seaweed was wrapped around my
head. To the roots of the mountains I sank down; the
earth beneath barred me in forever. But you, LORD
my God, brought my life up from the pit. When my
life was ebbing away, I remembered you, LORD, and
my prayer rose to you, to your holy temple. Those
who cling to worthless idols turn away from God's
love for them. But I, with shouts of grateful praise,
will sacrifice to you. What I have vowed I will make
good. I will say, 'Salvation comes from the LORD.' "

JONAH 2:4–9 NIV

- After Jonah ran away from God, he realized that God had never left His temple and would continue to hear his prayers. When have you struggled to believe that God is present to hear your prayers?

- When have your plans fallen apart? How did this impact your faith in God and your approach to prayer?

- Jonah turned to God in prayer with a confession of his failure. How are confession and repentance linked to prayer?

- This prayer offers a series of images of hopelessness and despair before trusting in God's help and deliverance. When have you felt hopeless or in a situation that was out of your depth?

- When has despair prevented you from approaching God in prayer? How does Jonah's prayer change the source of our hope?

- Jonah's prayer includes a striking image of people clinging to worthless idols, while those who trust in God are held by God's love. When have idols in your life promised security or prosperity only to let you down?

Father, You hold Your people in love and show mercy on them when they run away and choose their own plans over Your own. May we turn to You in our lowest moments of despair and trust that You can lift us out of the pit when all appears lost. May we turn toward You as You reign over the earth and promise new life and restoration for those who have turned away from You or trusted idols for their deliverance. Lead us to healing and restoration so that we can faithfully testify of Your mercy and praise You with grateful hearts. Amen.

ARE YOU READY TO RESPOND TO THE LORD?

Then the LORD called out again, "Samuel!" Again Samuel got up and went to Eli. "Here I am. Did you call me?" "I didn't call you, my son," Eli said. "Go back to bed." Samuel did not yet know the LORD because he had never had a message from the LORD before. So the LORD called a third time, and once more Samuel got up and went to Eli. "Here I am. Did you call me?" Then Eli realized it was the LORD who was calling the boy. So he said to Samuel, "Go and lie down again, and if someone calls again, say, 'Speak, LORD, your servant is listening.' " So Samuel went back to bed. And the LORD came and called as before, "Samuel! Samuel!" And Samuel replied, "Speak, your servant is listening."

1 SAMUEL 3:6–10 NLT

+ Is it possible that God is calling out to you today but you are not prepared to hear His voice? Are there ways that you can become more aware of God's call or more receptive to His message?

+ Are you expecting God to call out to you or to provide direction in your life? Are there reasons why you or people you know would be likely to doubt hearing from God?

+ Even when Samuel failed to recognize the voice of the Lord, God continued to call out to him until he responded. How does that speak to your experience of prayer?

- Are there people in your life who can provide guidance for how you pray? When have you struggled to pray because you lacked direction or wisdom to help you discern the voice of God with clarity and confidence?

- While many Christians see prayer as an opportunity to voice our thoughts with God, Samuel responded to God with silent attentiveness. How has silent listening to God impacted your prayer life? Are there ways you can make silence a more regular part of your prayer practices?

- Eli told Samuel to respond to God as a "servant." How does thinking of ourselves as servants impact the way we approach prayer?

Lord, You are always reaching out to Your people, waiting for them to respond to Your overtures. May we humbly wait for Your direction in silent expectation and act when we are confident of Your leading. Lead us away from distractions and doubts that keep us from prayer, and send wise guides to help us remain close to You and open to Your direction as we pray. Amen.

TAKE TIME TO CELEBRATE GOD'S DELIVERANCE

Then Moses and the sons of Israel sang this song to the LORD, and said, "I will sing to the LORD, for He is highly exalted; the horse and its rider He has hurled into the sea. The LORD is my strength and song, and He has become my salvation; this is my God, and I will praise Him; my father's God, and I will extol Him. The LORD is a warrior; the LORD is His name. Pharaoh's chariots and his army He has cast into the sea; and the choicest of his officers are drowned in the Red Sea. The deeps cover them; they went down into the depths like a stone. Your right hand, O LORD, is majestic in power, Your right hand, O LORD, shatters the enemy."

EXODUS 15:1–6 NASB

- A time of celebration and remembrance is an appropriate response to God's deliverance from danger or challenging circumstances. How can you celebrate and remember the ways God has been at work in your life and provided for you?

- How does gratitude impact the way you look back at your life? How does gratitude impact the way you view the future?

- It's easy to move quickly through life without seeing the ways God has been at work. If you could slow down this week, what might you notice about God?

- Are there problems or issues in your life that appear to be particularly daunting or challenging? Are there past experiences when God proved faithful that can help you look ahead in trust and courage?

• This song celebrates God's willingness to become involved in the struggles of His people. How does this knowledge impact the way you view God and approach prayer today?

• By celebrating God's deliverance, the Israelites were recognizing God's role in providing for them. How did this impact them as they faced future conflicts and tests?

Lord, we remember today that You are deeply concerned with Your people and choose to act on their behalf. You are faithful and powerful— able even to change the course of history. We celebrate Your provision and mercy in our lives and come to You with gratitude as we trust our lives in Your hands. Teach us to slow down and to take notice of the ways You are working around us, and may we always put our trust fully in You when we are in crisis. Amen.

TRUSTING GOD WITH OUR CHILDREN'S FUTURE

"For when you die and are buried with your ancestors, I will raise up one of your descendants, your own offspring, and I will make his kingdom strong. He is the one who will build a house—a temple—for my name. And I will secure his royal throne forever. I will be his father, and he will be my son. If he sins, I will correct and discipline him with the rod, like any father would do. But my favor will not be taken from him as I took it from Saul, whom I removed from your sight. Your house and your kingdom will continue before me for all time, and your throne will be secure forever."

2 SAMUEL 7:12-16 NLT

- Sometimes God says "no" to your prayers. In this case, God assured David that He had something far greater in mind than David had imagined. How have you felt when your prayers have gone unanswered? How does this passage speak to that?

- How do you view the future of your children? For instance, do you look forward in hope or are you weighed down with concerns?

- How are you preparing your children to rely on God and to seek God's path for their lives?

- God promised to raise up one of David's descendants and to make his kingdom strong. As you pray today, ask for God's protection and provision for your children and remain open to what God is saying to you.

- In what ways does God's promise to discipline David's son Solomon offer reassurance and hope to him as he prays?

- Much like a shepherd leads sheep with a rod toward safety and good choices, God promised to guide David's son and to correct him when necessary. What does that mean for your own role as a parent today?

- Parents must consider that one day they won't be around to guide and support their children. How does today's passage influence the way you think of preparing your children for the future? What would you want to change right now?

Father, I trust that You are present and stand prepared to correct and discipline Your people when needed. Today I entrust the future of my children to You and ask You to guide me in how to prepare them for a life of faith and obedience to Your commands. I ask You to help them take steps toward fulfilling Your will so that they won't lose their way or fall away from the blessings You readily give. Amen.

GOD NOTES OUR
TROUBLE AND GRIEF

Rise up, O LORD; O God, lift up your hand; do not forget the oppressed. Why do the wicked renounce God, and say in their hearts, "You will not call us to account"? But you do see! Indeed you note trouble and grief, that you may take it into your hands; the helpless commit themselves to you; you have been the helper of the orphan. Break the arm of the wicked and evildoers; seek out their wickedness until you find none. The LORD is king forever and ever; the nations shall perish from his land. O LORD, you will hear the desire of the meek; you will strengthen their heart, you will incline your ear to do justice for the orphan and the oppressed, so that those from earth may strike terror no more.

PSALM 10:12–18 NRSV

- Are you waiting for God to intervene or wondering where God is during a difficult situation? How does this psalm speak to you?

- Are there times when it appears that God has forgotten you? How does this psalm help you pray through seasons of uncertainty or suffering?

- The psalms often wrestle with the deferred justice of God while the wicked prosper. Is there space in your life today for lament? How would lament change the way you pray?

- The permanence of God is contrasted with the passing rule of kings and kingdoms. Does that bring comfort or tension for you today?

- A time of helplessness, need, or struggle is always difficult, but it is also an opportunity to depend on God more completely and to see His provision and presence. Has a difficult time proven helpful for you?

- God clearly takes the side of those who are powerless and suffering. Who are the people in your immediate area that you can pray for on a regular basis?

- God's future for the world is free from terror and suffering. What is your reaction to that?

Lord, You imagine a world where there is justice, peace, and provision for the needs of everyone. You have compassion on the hungry and hear the cries of those suffering injustice. All of creation waits for Your coming, which will end the turmoil of this world; but for today, give us courage to care for those in need and eyes to see those who desperately need our prayers. May we persevere when all appears lost and trust that You hear the cries of Your people. Amen.

TRUSTING IN GOD'S FAITHFULNESS

He said, "O LORD, the God of Israel, there is no God like You in heaven above or on earth beneath, keeping covenant and showing lovingkindness to Your servants who walk before You with all their heart, who have kept with Your servant, my father David, that which You have promised him; indeed, You have spoken with Your mouth and have fulfilled it with Your hand as it is this day. Now therefore, O LORD, the God of Israel, keep with Your servant David my father that which You have promised him, saying, 'You shall not lack a man to sit on the throne of Israel, if only your sons take heed to their way to walk before Me as you have walked.' "

1 KINGS 8:23–25 NASB

- Today's reading is part of a prayer for the dedication of the temple. Are there ways that prayer can become a more integral part of important events or rites of passage in your life?

- Solomon's prayer rested in the covenant of God with his father and in his confidence that God would remain faithful. Are there promises from God or experiences that give you confidence as you pray?

- The past events of God's faithfulness to David were an important part of Solomon's prayer. How does it help to begin prayer with remembering the past acts of God?

- Solomon benefitted from the legacy of David's faith and recounted it in detail during his own reign. How can you pass your faith, spiritual practices, or lessons from God to others?

- God's promises are certain and God is faithful, but obedience is central to seeing God's promises fulfilled. How does obedience tie in with prayer? Is there an area of your life that needs to be completely surrendered to God?

- Solomon did not live in obedience to the commands of God, and that resulted in future generations also drifting away from faith in the Lord. How can you take steps toward greater reliance on God and obedience to His commands?

Lord, You have promised that those who believe in Your Son and confess that He is Lord will belong to You. Help us to live in humble loyalty to You, trusting in Your promises, Your past faithful actions, and the hope we have in You. Protect us from temptation, forgive us when we choose our own way, and bring Your promises to fruition in our lives. Amen.

PRAY WITH CONFIDENCE IN GOD, NOT IN FEELINGS

Our actions will show that we belong to the truth, so we will be confident when we stand before God. Even if we feel guilty, God is greater than our feelings, and he knows everything. Dear friends, if we don't feel guilty, we can come to God with bold confidence. And we will receive from him whatever we ask because we obey him and do the things that please him. And this is his commandment: we must believe in the name of his Son, Jesus Christ, and love one another, just as he commanded us. Those who obey God's commandments remain in fellowship with him, and he with them. And we know he lives in us because the Spirit he gave us lives in us.

1 JOHN 3:19-24 NLT

- There will be emotional highs and lows as we seek God in prayer. Sometimes we may not feel like God is present or that our prayers are effective. How do you feel about prayer today?

- Guilt can derail prayer. Is there a feeling of guilt or shame that you have been carrying around? How would it change your prayers if you could believe that God is greater than your sins and guilty feelings?

- What would bold confidence look like for you as you approach God in prayer? How has Jesus made this kind of confidence possible?

- John wrote that obedience is an essential aspect of prayer, especially when it comes to petitions and requests. Why is obedience so important before we pray?

- John also wrote that we must "believe in the name of his Son" to live in obedience to God. What does it mean to believe in the name of Jesus? How is this related to prayer?

- Living in obedience ensures fellowship with God and awareness of the Holy Spirit in us. How does the Spirit provide assurance when our emotions or guilty thoughts afflict us in our prayers?

Jesus, You have removed our guilt, united us with God, and sent Your Spirit among us to provide comfort, healing, and assurance of Your presence. May we remain rooted in You, trusting in Your power and obedient to Your commands so that our wills and desires are aligned with Your will and Your kingdom. May we pray with confidence and hope as we learn to live in fellowship with You daily. Amen.

PRAYER LEADS TO ACTION

Then Peter replied, "I see very clearly that God shows no favoritism. In every nation he accepts those who fear him and do what is right. This is the message of Good News for the people of Israel—that there is peace with God through Jesus Christ, who is Lord of all. You know what happened throughout Judea, beginning in Galilee, after John began preaching his message of baptism. And you know that God anointed Jesus of Nazareth with the Holy Spirit and with power. Then Jesus went around doing good and healing all who were oppressed by the devil, for God was with him."

ACTS 10:34-38 NLT

+ Peter and Cornelius were in the habit of praying daily, so it's likely that they didn't have visions or angelic visitors each time they sat down to pray. What does this story teach us about perseverance in prayer and waiting on God?

+ Peter and Cornelius acted immediately after God met them in prayer. How has obedience been linked to prayer in your own life?

+ Why was the message of God not showing favoritism so revolutionary? What does this reveal about God's character?

+ Have you struggled to believe that God accepts you and hears your prayers? What did Peter have to say about gaining God's acceptance?

+ Peter shared that there is peace with God through Jesus Christ, who is Lord of all. How does recognizing the lordship of Christ bring peace to your life? Is there an area of your life where you need to submit your desires or plans to the lordship of Christ?

- The Holy Spirit was important in the ministry of Jesus and in the life of the early Church. What have you believed about the Holy Spirit? Does Peter challenge you to step out in faith in any new ways?

- How does the presence of God change the day-to-day actions of Christians?

Jesus, You are the Lord of all and offer Your Holy Spirit to all who receive You and live in obedience to Your commands. You hear the prayers of Your people and promise to show up faithfully for those who patiently wait for You. Restore us when we choose our own path, and guide us to live in faithful obedience that brings blessings to others. May we fully participate in the presence of Your Holy Spirit and serve out of the Spirit's power. Amen.

GOD'S PLAN FOR INSTRUCTING CHILDREN

These words, which I am commanding you today,
shall be on your heart. You shall teach them diligently
to your sons and shall talk of them when you sit in
your house and when you walk by the way and when
you lie down and when you rise up. You shall bind
them as a sign on your hand and they shall be as
frontals on your forehead. You shall write them on
the doorposts of your house and on your gates.

DEUTERONOMY 6:6–9 NASB

+ How can some of the habits that you find most helpful
  for remembering something help you become more
  aware of the Lord and keep these commandments
  on your heart?

+ Are there times when your children are especially
  receptive to conversations and new ideas? How can
  you use some of that time to talk about what the
  Lord is teaching you?

+ The idea of "repeating" these commands diligently
  to your children and speaking of them even when
  sitting down, lying down, or walking suggests that
  this is an ongoing, repetitive process of discipleship.
  How can you make it easier to speak about the Lord's
  teachings on a regular basis?

+ The Lord's approach to instructing children may
  appear demanding and time consuming. What are
  the opportunities and challenges of making a regular

practice of talking about these commandments and instructions so often?

- ♦ How can you ensure that the words of scripture are on your heart in the days to come?

- ♦ Consider the moments in your day when you can talk about scripture with your children. When can you most likely have a conversation like this?

- ♦ Assuming you won't tie Bible verses to your head or write them on your doorpost, what are some modern ways to make scripture more visible for yourself?

Father, help me to become more aware of how I spend my time each day, and guide me in ways to make scripture more visible and more memorable. Help me to see ways I can place Your words on my heart and how I can take advantage of every opportunity to discuss Your words of life with my children. May Your words rest on their hearts as well so that they grow to treasure them and to obey them, keeping them ever before them throughout their days. And may they also talk about Your commands and Your salvation throughout their days with future generations. Amen.

LEARNING TO WAIT PATIENTLY FOR GOD

As for me, I look to the LORD for help. I wait confidently for God to save me, and my God will certainly hear me. Do not gloat over me, my enemies! For though I fall, I will rise again. Though I sit in darkness, the LORD will be my light. I will be patient as the LORD punishes me, for I have sinned against him. But after that, he will take up my case and give me justice for all I have suffered from my enemies. The LORD will bring me into the light, and I will see his righteousness. Then my enemies will see that the LORD is on my side. They will be ashamed that they taunted me, saying, "So where is the LORD— that God of yours?" With my own eyes I will see their downfall; they will be trampled like mud in the streets.

MICAH 7:7-10 NLT

* Where do people typically look for help in their lives? Where are you looking for help today? What would it look like if you turned to God alone as your source of help?

* Before turning to God for help, Micah dealt with the sins that had prevented him from experiencing intimacy with God. He even believed that God was punishing him for his sins. Is there a need for confession and restoration in your life before approaching God in prayer?

* Are there times when disobedience has gotten in the way of your prayers? How does Micah's prayer move from repentance to restoration?

- What does restoration look like for God's people?

- While Micah waited on God, he endured taunts and discouragement. What makes waiting on God difficult for you? Are there people who have made comments that contradict Micah's experience?

- What are some of the doubts that you've had about God during prayer? How does facing doubt relate to waiting patiently on God in prayer?

Lord, we face doubts and conflict that call Your attentiveness and presence into question. You have made redemption and new life possible in Jesus, restoring us to a right relationship with You despite these voices that call You into question. Help us to trust in You and Your restoration as we confess our sins and learn to wait on You. May we see the fulfillment of Your promises and share about Your saving help with others. Amen.

ASK FOR GOD'S HELP

Make me to know your ways, O LORD; teach me your paths. Lead me in your truth, and teach me, for you are the God of my salvation; for you I wait all day long. Be mindful of your mercy, O LORD, and of your steadfast love, for they have been from of old. Do not remember the sins of my youth or my transgressions; according to your steadfast love remember me, for your goodness' sake, O LORD! Good and upright is the LORD; therefore he instructs sinners in the way. He leads the humble in what is right, and teaches the humble his way. All the paths of the LORD are steadfast love and faithfulness, for those who keep his covenant and his decrees.

PSALM 25:4-10 NRSV

- When have you found Christianity challenging or even mysterious? That's no surprise for the writers of the psalms. Their solution was to ask for God's wisdom and direction. What can you ask God to show you today?

- Relying on God's teaching and direction is a major commitment that the writer of this psalm waited for all day long. What would that kind of waiting look like in your life? Is there a particular issue where you need God's instruction?

- Do you try to approach God based on your own virtues and accomplishments or on God's goodness and mercy? How does self-reliance undermine your relationship with God or your ability to pray?

- Are there sins that you carry with you or burdens of guilt that make it difficult to pray? How does this psalm suggest dealing with these feelings or memories?

- If God is eager to instruct sinners and to teach them in His ways, humility is one of the main requirements for spiritual practices that connect us with God. Where in your life have you seen a need for humility?

- God remains faithful to those who obey His commands. Is that challenging or comforting for you? Why?

Father, You sent Jesus to reveal the Way, the Truth, and the Life, and so I ask You to guide me into Your will today. On the basis of Your mercy and good pleasure, I trust that You are present and willing to guide me into Your truth so that I can live in obedience to Your commands. Lead me into the security and hope of Your steadfast love. Amen.

ENCOURAGEMENT TO
A HIGHER CALLING

*You remember our labor and toil, brothers and sisters;
we worked night and day, so that we might not burden
any of you while we proclaimed to you the gospel
of God. You are witnesses, and God also, how pure,
upright, and blameless our conduct was toward you
believers. As you know, we dealt with each one of you
like a father with his children, urging and encouraging
you and pleading that you lead a life worthy of God,
who calls you into his own kingdom and glory.*

1 Thessalonians 2:9–12 NRSV

- Paul worked exceptionally hard to avoid placing any kind of barrier between the Gospel message and the Thessalonians. How can you make sure you communicate the Gospel as clearly as possible to your children?

- What may prevent your children from responding to the Gospel message today? Are these barriers truly essential for the message, and can you help alleviate them?

- When Paul considered his conduct in front of the Thessalonians, he was especially aware that being pure, upright, and blameless impacted how seriously they took his message. How could your behavior either confirm or undermine the Gospel message for your children?

- The vision Paul casts for his treatment of the Thessalonians is an encouraging and kind father who urges and pleads with his children to live worthy of God. Are you more likely to encourage or discourage your children? How can you make sure they feel encouraged in their faith?

- How did your own father treat you? Do you see those past dynamics showing up in your relationship with your children? Take a moment to pray, thanking God for the good things your father modeled, forgiving your father's failures, and asking God to help you carry the best parts of your father to your children.

- The reason for Paul's exhortations to the Thessalonians is the higher calling into God's kingdom and glory. How can you remind your children of this high calling to be with God in holiness and glory, even if the thought of that may feel unobtainable today?

Father, I thank You for the model that Paul set before the Thessalonians and his commitment to never block them from receiving the Gospel message. May I also share Your message of life, hope, and love with my children in such a way that they remain open to You and Your love for them. May they choose to follow You toward the glory of Your kingdom rather than the passing things of this world. Amen.

WE ENTER PRAYER
WITH LAMENT

How long, O LORD? Will you forget me forever? How long will you hide your face from me? How long must I bear pain in my soul, and have sorrow in my heart all day long? How long shall my enemy be exalted over me? Consider and answer me, O LORD my God! Give light to my eyes, or I will sleep the sleep of death, and my enemy will say, "I have prevailed"; my foes will rejoice because I am shaken. But I trusted in your steadfast love; my heart shall rejoice in your salvation. I will sing to the LORD, because he has dealt bountifully with me.

PSALM 13:1-6 NRSV

- If you are bearing doubts or frustrations toward God today, how could you put them into words as you pray?

- Laments are an important aspect of the psalms, revealing that the writers of inspired scripture valued honesty about their doubt, fear, and confusion. How could today's lament apply to a time in your life? Are you in a season of lament?

- How are prayers of lament viewed in your church? How can you help others speak words of lament when they pray? How can you support others in their pain and frustrations with God?

- When you have suffered or felt ridiculed by others, what do you imagine God thinks of your circumstance? Has that made you more or less likely to pray to God?

- The psalmist found comfort in God's steadfast love in a time of trouble. Where does your mind go in a time of trouble or suffering? How does meditating on God's steadfast love bring comfort or resolution to your life today?

- Worship is another appropriate response in a time of uncertainty because it puts God in His proper place. Is there a form of worship that you particularly relate to? How can worship become part of your response to a challenging time?

God, You see my suffering and my weakness. You see those who wish ill upon Your people, and You are never far away from me. Show Yourself strong and faithful when I am afflicted and uncertain. May those who feel hopeless or far away from You gain a glimpse of You and Your steadfast love as well. Teach me to pray with an open, honest mind, sharing my thoughts with You, but may Your revelation and presence overcome any sorrow or doubts that come to mind. Amen.

HOLY LIVING DOESN'T HAPPEN BY MISTAKE

"You shall therefore impress these words of mine on your heart and on your soul; and you shall bind them as a sign on your hand, and they shall be as frontals on your forehead. You shall teach them to your sons, talking of them when you sit in your house and when you walk along the road and when you lie down and when you rise up. You shall write them on the doorposts of your house and on your gates, so that your days and the days of your sons may be multiplied on the land which the LORD swore to your fathers to give them, as long as the heavens remain above the earth."

DEUTERONOMY 11:18-21 NASB

+ Holiness is essential for anyone who would approach God in prayer, but it requires intentionally creating space for God to work in your life. Which spiritual practices have been most life-giving for you?

+ This passage suggests putting scripture in visible places and making it a regular part of daily conversations and relationships. How can you become more aware of scripture and more receptive to its message today?

+ Why would God command His people to place scripture on public places such as their doorposts and gates? Is there a lesson for you in how you practice your faith in public?

+ Do you find it easier to meditate on scripture early in the morning when you rise or late in the evening when you go to bed? Are there benefits of incorporating meditation into those particular points each day?

- For those who aren't impressing scripture on their heart and soul, what could be impressing itself on their heart and soul instead? Are there particular distractions or ways of thinking that compete in your heart and soul against the influence of scripture?

- What are the results of making scripture a more integral part of your daily practices?

Lord, You have given us the gift of scripture to guide all people into loving relationship with You and to reveal Your love. May I make space each day to meditate on Your words, and may Your message take root in my daily decisions and relationships. Lead me to greater awareness of You, love for neighbors, and faithfulness to Your commands as Your life-giving words drown out any other influence in my life. Amen.

PRAYER IS
PERSISTENT IN HOPE

Because I love Zion, I will not keep still. Because my heart yearns for Jerusalem, I cannot remain silent. I will not stop praying for her until her righteousness shines like the dawn, and her salvation blazes like a burning torch. The nations will see your righteousness. World leaders will be blinded by your glory. And you will be given a new name by the LORD's own mouth. The LORD will hold you in his hand for all to see—a splendid crown in the hand of God. . . . Your children will commit themselves to you, O Jerusalem, just as a young man commits himself to his bride. Then God will rejoice over you as a bridegroom rejoices over his bride.

ISAIAH 62:1-3, 5 NLT

- Have you ever struggled to keep praying for a situation that appeared hopeless? What encouraged you to continue praying?

- Intercession can have a powerful impact on high-stakes situations. Is there a situation today that you can intercede for?

- In a time of failure or struggle, what do you imagine God intends for your restoration? Do you believe that God desires to rejoice over you and to see you fully restored?

- How does imagining God holding you in His hand impact the way you pray? Is there a reason why imagining that may be difficult at this point in your life?

- What kind of identity do you imagine for yourself right now? What could it look like for God to give you a new identity?

- Any healing that may come to God's people will be a result of their commitment to live obediently. What do you think that kind of commitment looks like? Are there ways that the imagery of a marriage commitment helps you?

- The Bible often uses marriage imagery to describe God's relationship with His people. Take time to consider what that kind of joy may look like as you approach God in prayer.

Lord, You desire to redeem Your people, restoring them and bringing healing into their lives. May I remain committed and vigilant, praying to You and interceding for myself and for others until You have intervened in my life with Your power and presence. May I find rest in the identity You give to me and a renewed desire to live in obedience. May I find new life where there had once been a loss of hope. Amen.

HOW TO TAKE REFUGE IN GOD

Protect me, O God, for in you I take refuge. I say to the LORD, "You are my Lord; I have no good apart from you." As for the holy ones in the land, they are the noble, in whom is all my delight. Those who choose another god multiply their sorrows; their drink offerings of blood I will not pour out or take their names upon my lips. The LORD is my chosen portion and my cup; you hold my lot. The boundary lines have fallen for me in pleasant places; I have a goodly heritage. I bless the LORD who gives me counsel; in the night also my heart instructs me. I keep the LORD always before me; because he is at my right hand, I shall not be moved. Therefore my heart is glad, and my soul rejoices; my body also rests secure.

PSALM 16:1–9 NRSV

- When you think of God as a refuge, what do you imagine? Are there other places where you have taken refuge?

- When have you seen your sorrows or the sorrows of someone else multiplied by relying on something or someone other than God?

- How can you make God a source of security and satisfaction today? What would it look like to trust God with your provision and future well-being?

- This psalm offers the assurance that trusting in God is beneficial and hopeful for the future. How do you see today's consumer culture and its obsession with affluence running counter to the contentment found in the boundary lines and inheritance that God grants?

- In what ways have you received counsel from God? How can you make more space to receive direction and stability from God?

- Take a moment to imagine that God is before you, holding you firm. How does this influence the way you think of your day? How can you continue to keep God "before" you today?

Lord, teach me to rely on Your wisdom and to accept what comes from Your hand. May I rest in You and You alone today, trusting You to guide me and to provide what I need at the right time. Help me to step more completely into the life of faith that You have marked out for me each day, and may I rejoice in the rest that You give. Amen.

WHAT DO WE IMAGINE ABOUT GOD'S LOVE?

For this reason I kneel before the Father, from whom every family in heaven and on earth derives its name. I pray that out of his glorious riches he may strengthen you with power through his Spirit in your inner being, so that Christ may dwell in your hearts through faith. And I pray that you, being rooted and established in love, may have power, together with all the Lord's holy people, to grasp how wide and long and high and deep is the love of Christ, and to know this love that surpasses knowledge—that you may be filled to the measure of all the fullness of God. Now to him who is able to do immeasurably more than all we ask or imagine, according to his power that is at work within us, to him be glory in the church and in Christ Jesus throughout all generations, for ever and ever! Amen.

Ephesians 3:14–21 niv

- Before you begin to pray today, consider how Paul described God as the Father. Every family on earth comes from the Father. Are your prayers changed if you imagine God deeply invested and tied up in who you are and where you come from?

- God's resources are deep and plentiful, so asking God for greater spiritual strength is not getting water from a stone. Assuming that the Spirit is already present in your life, is there any reason why you wouldn't feel confident to ask for Christ to dwell in your heart by faith?

- God's power is at work in you today, and even better, God can do more in your life than you can ask or imagine. What would it look like to take a leap of faith in asking God to work in your life?

- Do you find it comforting to know that the love of Christ for you surpasses knowledge? How does this unfathomable love of Christ impact how you pray today?

- Each day you are most likely being filled with one thing or another. Are there things that compete with God to fill you? What would it look like to begin to be filled to the fullness of God?

Father, You have sent Your Spirit to dwell within Your people and have graced them with Your compassion and mercy. May I begin to experience the fullness of Your love, and may Christ take root in my life so that I can share Your goodness with others. May Your fullness overflow in my life to those I meet today. Amen.

WE PRAY FOR GOD'S RESTORATION

For I know my transgressions, and my sin is ever before me. Against you, you alone, have I sinned, and done what is evil in your sight, so that you are justified in your sentence and blameless when you pass judgment. Indeed, I was born guilty, a sinner when my mother conceived me. You desire truth in the inward being; therefore teach me wisdom in my secret heart. . . . Hide your face from my sins, and blot out all my iniquities. Create in me a clean heart, O God, and put a new and right spirit within me. Do not cast me away from your presence, and do not take your holy spirit from me. Restore to me the joy of your salvation, and sustain in me a willing spirit.

PSALM 51:3-6, 9-12 NRSV

- Is there a particular sin that is on your mind today as you enter into prayer? How do you typically handle a lingering sense of guilt over a particular sin?

- What does confession of sin look like in this passage? How can you move toward reconciliation with God through confession? How does God desire to deal with the guilt of His people?

- God does not abandon His people in their sins. How can you pray to God about your sins based on this passage?

- While some may try to cleanse themselves before approaching God in prayer, how does this passage suggest coming to God? What role do you have to play in your restoration if God is creating a clean heart and renewing a right spirit in you?

- As you imagine what it looks like to live a life of obedience before God rather than a life of disobedience and guilt, what does it mean to live with a "willing spirit"?

- You have been saved from sin, but do you live as if that is true? Do you need to ask God to restore joy in the reality of your salvation?

God, You see my failures and You know my secret sins, and yet You desire to bring renewal and restoration in my life so that my joy in Your salvation may be complete. Reveal the ways I have departed from Your path of life, and lead me to Your truth. May Your Spirit cleanse and sustain me so that I delight in Your laws and live in unity with You. Amen.

LIVING BY FAITH
BRINGS STABILITY

This is what the LORD says: "Cursed is the one who trust in man, who draws strength from mere flesh and whose heart turns away from the LORD. That person will be like a bush in the wastelands; they will not see prosperity when it comes. They will dwell in the parched places of the desert, in a salt land where no one lives. But blessed is the one who trusts in the LORD, whose confidence is in him. They will be like a tree planted by the water that sends out its roots by the stream. It does not fear when heat comes; its leaves are always green. It has no worries in a year of drought and never fails to bear fruit." The heart is deceitful above all things and beyond cure. Who can understand it? "I the LORD search the heart and examine the mind, to reward each person according to their conduct, according to what their deeds deserve."

JEREMIAH 17:5-10 NIV

* Where do you draw strength from most days? What would it look like to draw your strength from the Lord and to turn your heart fully to the Lord in faith?

* There are two images in this passage: one for those who live by faith and one for those who trust in man. Does one relate to your life more than the other right now? What do you want to pray about in response?

* If the heart is deceitful, what does it look like to depend on the heart rather than on God? How can

you take a step in faith today rather than relying on your heart?

- While it may be unsettling to imagine that God is searching your heart and fully aware of what's on your mind, it can also be a comfort if you are uncertain or have afflictive thoughts. How can you offer your thoughts to God and trust Him to work in them for your benefit?

- There is an element of reward and punishment in the Bible, and your actions will result in either positive or negative consequences. How does this impact the way you live in obedience or disobedience today?

Lord, I confess that I have relied on my own wisdom and on the opinions of other people. May I be rooted in You as I place all my confidence in Your presence and power in my life. Guide me to the right thoughts and actions so that I remain fully rooted in You and can stand before You in purity and uprightness. Amen.

A GOOD MEMORY LEADS TO COURAGE AND FAITH

"But I said to you, 'Don't be shocked or afraid of them! The LORD your God is going ahead of you. He will fight for you, just as you saw him do in Egypt. And you saw how the LORD your God cared for you all along the way as you traveled through the wilderness, just as a father cares for his child. Now he has brought you to this place.' But even after all he did, you refused to trust the LORD your God, who goes before you looking for the best places to camp, guiding you with a pillar of fire by night and a pillar of cloud by day."

DEUTERONOMY 1:29-33 NLT

- While the people of Israel looked ahead at the many challenges before them, why would the Lord ask them to look back at their past?

- Fear is a natural response to difficult circumstances. What kind of reassurance does God offer to Israel so that they can respond with courage and faith?

- You may have passed through a difficult "wilderness" season where everything felt like a struggle or the future remained uncertain. Based on today's passage, what are the potential benefits of a wilderness season?

- Consider something that shocks you or causes you fear today. How can the Lord's guidance to Israel help you respond with faith and courage?

- Living by faith doesn't mean avoiding conflict. The Lord even assured the people of Israel that they had been brought to where they were. Consider your own conflicts and where God is present even in the midst of them.

- God is compared to a caring father who provides for his child. How does your role as a father shape the way you view God's care and concern for you?

- Why did Israel initially fail to trust God's provision and protection? What are your greatest challenges in living by faith today?

Help me, Lord, to remember Your past faithfulness and provision in the challenges and uncertainties of life. When I am shocked and afraid, help me to remember that You have guided me in the past and that You will not abandon or forsake me. May the compassion and care that I have for my children guide how I view Your love for me. You have been faithful in the past, and You will continue to be present throughout the challenges of my life. Amen.

BE DISCIPLINED AND PREPARED FOR PRAYER

The end of all things is near; therefore, be of sound judgment and sober spirit for the purpose of prayer. Above all, keep fervent in your love for one another, because love covers a multitude of sins. Be hospitable to one another without complaint. As each one has received a special gift, employ it in serving one another as good stewards of the manifold grace of God. Whoever speaks, is to do so as one who is speaking the utterances of God; whoever serves is to do so as one who is serving by the strength which God supplies; so that in all things God may be glorified through Jesus Christ, to whom belongs the glory and dominion forever and ever. Amen.

1 PETER 4:7-11 NASB

* Nothing is permanent in this world, so whether the Lord returns soon or tarries, the one guarantee is change. How can you remain disciplined and prepared to pray while facing so much uncertainty?

* Why do you think Peter emphasized commitment to fervently love others, even when facing an uncertain future and the hostility of some in the world? Why is it essential for love to cover a multitude of sins?

* Peter said that each Christian has been given a special gift from God that can be used to serve others. Take some time to consider what your gift may be, or, if you know what your gift is, consider how you can use it effectively.

- What does it look like for you to serve with the strength that God supplies? Consider bringing your service opportunities to God in prayer and asking Him to provide what you need to serve others well.

- What are the risks of serving others in your own strength and by relying on your own resources?

- Why is God-empowered service so important at a tumultuous time in history, especially since Peter anticipated that the end is near?

Jesus, You gave Your people wisdom and power through the gift of the Holy Spirit, and You commanded us to love our neighbors as ourselves. May I make space to pray this week so that I am mindful of You, am aware of my weaknesses, and learn to trust more completely in Your presence and strength. May I serve others with the grace You have given to me and encourage them to pursue You with all their heart. Amen.

SEEKING WHAT ONLY GOD CAN GIVE

At that time Jesus, full of joy through the Holy Spirit, said, "I praise you, Father, Lord of heaven and earth, because you have hidden these things from the wise and learned, and revealed them to little children. Yes, Father, for this is what you were pleased to do. All things have been committed to me by my Father. No one knows who the Son is except the Father, and no one knows who the Father is except the Son and those to whom the Son chooses to reveal him." Then he turned to his disciples and said privately, "Blessed are the eyes that see what you see. For I tell you that many prophets and kings wanted to see what you see but did not see it, and to hear what you hear but did not hear it."

LUKE 10:21-24 NIV

- ✦ Jesus began His prayer with praise for God the Father. Is there something that you are grateful for or that you can thank God for as you pray today?

- ✦ When describing the kingdom of God, Jesus told His followers that they must become like little children to enter it. How can you more fully embrace this kind of childlike faith as you pray?

- ✦ What does it mean that all things have been committed to Jesus by the Father? How does a promise as sweeping as this impact the way you pray or make requests to God?

- There is nothing that anyone can do to change what they see of God's revelation. The experience of God is wholly dependent on God's grace. In what ways could this be a liberating message for you in your pursuit of God?

- Just as some people longed to experience God more directly only to find that it wasn't the right time for that revelation, you may find that the timing isn't right for your prayer requests. How does this insight impact the way you make requests during prayer?

Father, You delight in those who have a childlike faith and who depend on You just like a little child. Grant me the patience to wait for Your direction and the wisdom to discern Your voice as I pray. I trust that Jesus has been given all wisdom and power, and I trust that He will care for me as a member of His family. Amen.

CONFESS FAILURE TO A COMPASSIONATE FATHER

"But when he came to himself he said, 'How many of my father's hired hands have bread enough and to spare, but here I am dying of hunger! I will get up and go to my father, and I will say to him, "Father, I have sinned against heaven and before you; I am no longer worthy to be called your son; treat me like one of your hired hands.' " So he set off and went to his father. But while he was still far off, his father saw him and was filled with compassion; he ran and put his arms around him and kissed him."

LUKE 15:17–20 NRSV

- Why had the prodigal son resisted returning to his father initially? Why would you resist hiding your failures from God or not confessing your faults?

- What did it take for the prodigal son to realize the severity of his circumstances? Are there signs right now in your life or in your past that indicate a need for God's forgiveness and restoration?

- What do you notice about the son's confession and the way he understood his sin? What does it say about both the seriousness of sin and the depths of God's compassion?

- In what ways did the son need to change before he was ready to return to his father?

- Based on what the son prepared to say to his father, what kind of reception did he expect from his father?

What kind of response do you expect from God when you think of confessing your faults?

• How does this story challenge you to show compassion and forgiveness to your children when they have done something wrong?

• Are there reasons why your children may be hesitant to right a wrong with you or to speak about their failures with you? How may the son's expectations and the father's example relate to your relationships with your children today?

Father, help me to move past the shame of my failures so that I can fully embrace Your forgiveness and kindness. May Your love and compassion shape me so that I will come to You in faith, confidence, and hope, trusting that I can never lose my position as Your beloved son. As I share that same compassion and kindness with my children, may they always feel safe and secure sharing their faults and failures with me so that they will never have anything to fear in our relationship. Amen.

GOD DESIRES LOVING OBEDIENCE

*For twenty-three years—from the thirteenth year
of Josiah son of Amon king of Judah until this very
day—the word of the LORD has come to me and I
have spoken to you again and again, but you have
not listened. And though the LORD has sent all his
servants the prophets to you again and again, you
have not listened or paid any attention. They said,
"Turn now, each of you, from your evil ways and
your evil practices, and you can stay in the land the
LORD gave to you and your ancestors for ever and
ever. Do not follow other gods to serve and worship
them; do not arouse my anger with what your hands
have made. Then I will not harm you." "But you
did not listen to me," declares the LORD, "and you
have aroused my anger with what your hands have
made, and you have brought harm to yourselves."*

JEREMIAH 25:3-7 NIV

* Is there a warning or a message about your life
  choices that God has been sending to you in this
  season of life? How can ignoring warning signs from
  God impact the life of faith?

* If you are living in disobedience, what are some
  ways you can turn away from sin and begin to
  wholeheartedly pursue God and His will?

* Idols are things you can easily control because you've
  created them yourself. Are there idols in your life

that promise deliverance but end up alienating you from God?

- ◆ God is very patient with His people, but His patience has a limit. How does this consequence impact the way you approach obedience and prayer?

- ◆ The Bible often holds in tension God's mercy and judgment. Are you more likely to emphasize one or the other? Is there an event, experience, or teaching that has influenced that emphasis?

- ◆ After a long period of disobedience, how does God hope His people will respond to His overtures to return to Him?

Lord, You long for me to view myself as one of Your treasured people. Deliver me from the temptations I face and the failures of my past. Cleanse me of my sins so that I can approach You in purity and confidence, free to listen to Your voice and to make choices that bring You glory. May my life become a testimony of Your reconciliation and redemptive power. Amen.

JESUS HELPS US WHEN WE DOUBT

They brought the boy to Him. When he saw Him, immediately the spirit threw him into a convulsion, and falling to the ground, he began rolling around and foaming at the mouth. And He asked his father, "How long has this been happening to him?" And he said, "From childhood. It has often thrown him both into the fire and into the water to destroy him. But if You can do anything, take pity on us and help us!" And Jesus said to him, " 'If You can?' All things are possible to him who believes." Immediately the boy's father cried out and said, "I do believe; help my unbelief."

MARK 9:20–24 NASB

- The father in today's passage felt desperate and completely unable to help his son. How have you felt about God when you are in a difficult situation like this?

- A father can feel especially vulnerable and even powerless when his child is in danger or suffering in some way. How did Jesus respond to the father's plea for help?

- When you imagine how Jesus cares for your children, how does it match up with the way Jesus responded to the father and son in today's story?

- In what ways do you see yourself in the father in today's passage? How do you feel different from the father in this passage?

- The father admits his struggles with doubt even as he proclaims his belief. Even with the admission of doubt, Jesus healed his child. What does this passage teach you about doubt and belief?

- When you are facing a crisis, especially with your children, where do you imagine God is at as you face uncertainty?

- If you brought your own child to Jesus in the midst of a crisis, how do you imagine Jesus responding?

- What does this passage teach you about faith and parenting?

Jesus, I trust that You care deeply for me and for my children. You see my doubts, fears, and uncertainties, and You still welcome me in your presence. May I never stand back from You in fear or doubt so that I can't trust You to bring healing and restoration. Help my faith to stand strong even when I am facing my worst fears and anxieties. And may my children remain safe and grow strong in their faith so that they learn to trust in Your compassion and power. I trust You with the care of my family. Amen.

PREPARE FOR PRAYER WITH SCRIPTURE

*How can young people keep their way pure?
By guarding it according to your word. With my
whole heart I seek you; do not let me stray from
your commandments. I treasure your word in my
heart, so that I may not sin against you. Blessed
are you, O LORD; teach me your statutes. With my
lips I declare all the ordinances of your mouth.
I delight in the way of your decrees as much as
in all riches. I will meditate on your precepts,
and fix my eyes on your ways. I will delight in
your statutes; I will not forget your word.*

PSALM 119:9–16 NRSV

+ What does it look like to seek God with your whole heart? Is there something you may do differently today to seek God with your whole heart?

+ Purity and obedience to the commands of God are viewed throughout scripture as essential for prayer. What does this psalm suggest so that you can remain fixed on God's way for your life?

+ One of the guards against sin is treasuring God's Word in your heart. What are you carrying in your heart today? Is there something that is pulling you away from God's direction in your life? Can you take a step to hold God's Word in your heart?

+ Speaking God's Word over your life is another way to remain secure in God's direction. Are there contexts where you can speak about the promises of God and the words of scripture?

- Are you meditating on the scriptures that show you God's ways? How can this help you with your approach to daily prayer?

- If you're struggling to live in obedience or to pray regularly, consider making a request for God's help to learn His statutes. How would this kind of request change your approach to prayer?

Support me, Lord, in the daily disciplines and practices that will help me live in prayerful obedience to Your teachings. Instruct me in Your ways, open my eyes to the wisdom of Your words in scripture, and make space in my life each day so that I can rest fully in Your teachings. May Your wisdom and truth guide me away from all that would distract or send me off course, so that I can serve You without hindrance. Amen.

SURRENDER TO CHRIST AND GAIN YOUR SOUL

Then Jesus said to his disciples, "If any of you wants to be my follower, you must give up your own way, take up your cross, and follow me. If you try to hang on to your life, you will lose it. But if you give up your life for my sake, you will save it. And what do you benefit if you gain the whole world but lose your own soul? Is anything worth more than your soul? For the Son of Man will come with his angels in the glory of his Father and will judge all people according to their deeds. And I tell you the truth, some standing here right now will not die before they see the Son of Man coming in his Kingdom."

MATTHEW 16:24-28 NLT

- What has been your "own way" of life that has conflicted with following Christ?

- Which parts of your own way have you surrendered already? What are the costs of that? Are there parts of your own way that remain difficult to give up?

- The irony of giving up your life to follow Christ is that you can't hold on to it forever anyway. If the only reason to hold on to your life is for short-term reasons, how does this long view of surrender to Christ impact your priorities today?

- What is your understanding of your soul? How does this passage help you safeguard your soul?

- While God is merciful and desires to help His people live in obedience to His commands, there will be a judgment for what all people have done and what they have failed to do. How does the thought of giving an account for your actions impact you? Does this lend an urgency to your prayers today?

Jesus, reveal the divisions in my heart, the misplaced priorities of my life, and the ways that I am holding myself back from You. Open my eyes to the wisdom of Your commandments, and direct my focus to the power of Your Holy Spirit in my life. May I turn away from the pleasures and profits of today so that I can entrust myself to You, seeking Your nourishment and redemption in my soul. May I delight in Your ways so that I can stand before You in confidence one day. Amen.

YOU ARE ADOPTED BY GOD

But when the right time came, God sent his Son, born of a woman, subject to the law. God sent him to buy freedom for us who were slaves to the law, so that he could adopt us as his very own children. And because we are his children, God has sent the Spirit of his Son into our hearts, prompting us to call out, "Abba, Father." Now you are no longer a slave but God's own child. And since you are his child, God has made you his heir.

GALATIANS 4:4-7 NLT

+ Paul speaks of Jesus coming at the "right time." How does this moment in your life feel right now? Where are you content and at peace? What is causing you fear or frustration?

+ How do you feel about God right now? Do you feel that God is a parent to you or some other authority figure who holds you at arm's length?

+ What is the significance of Jesus placing Himself under the law and living in obedience to it? How does that impact you personally?

+ If you're no longer a slave to the law and are now adopted into God's family, what does that mean for your daily decisions and choices?

+ How can the arrival of God's Spirit in your heart change how you see yourself? How does the Holy Spirit dwelling in your heart change how you live in obedience as God's child?

- As a father, how do you make sure your child feels safe and secure? How does God bring that same sense of safety and security to you?

- How does being adopted into God's family influence how you pray and read the Bible? When it's hard to pray, how could awareness of this passage help?

- When you think of the ways you care for your children, how does that shape the way you imagine God treating you?

- Are there ways that you can model God's acceptance, generosity, and forgiveness when parenting your children?

Jesus, thank You for placing Yourself under the law and enduring the trials and tribulations of our world alongside us. May I live in the freedom of the Holy Spirit who is at work in my life and who empowers me to remain attentive and obedient to Your will. May I remain aware of Your presence that is with me at just the right time, even if I may have doubts and uncertainties. Help me to live in the comfort and assurance that You have adopted me into Your family and that You can never leave or forsake me. Amen.

LIVE BY FAITH IN ALL SEASONS OF ADVERSITY

"But I say to you who hear, love your enemies, do good to those who hate you, bless those who curse you, pray for those who mistreat you. Whoever hits you on the cheek, offer him the other also; and whoever takes away your coat, do not withhold your shirt from him either. Give to everyone who asks of you, and whoever takes away what is yours, do not demand it back. Treat others the same way you want them to treat you. If you love those who love you, what credit is that to you? For even sinners love those who love them. If you do good to those who do good to you, what credit is that to you? For even sinners do the same."

LUKE 6:27–33 NASB

- Each example in this passage is a kind of adversity. Which of these commands do you find most difficult to put into practice?

- What would it look like to entrust the most challenging of these commands to God? How can you pray about the issues brought up in this passage, whether finances, possessions, or a personal sense of worth?

- Jesus spoke as if there were a higher priority in treating enemies and sinners well, noting that there is no "reward" for being kind to those who are kind to you. What do you think it means to be credited by God for loving enemies?

- How can prayer prepare you to be generous to those in need or kind to those who are combative or offensive?

- How would you live differently if you vowed to always give to those who asked for financial help and were in need?

- Are there responses to poverty, violence, or incivility that have become ingrained in our culture and run counter to the teachings of Jesus? How can you pray about living in obedience to the commands of Jesus today?

Jesus, You forgave Your betrayer, executioners, and mockers as You died on the cross. Help me to love my enemies and to be generous with the resources You have entrusted to me when others ask for assistance. Guide me away from retaliation and anger when I am mistreated or when I encounter a difficult situation. May I respond with the mercy You have shown me and with faith that You can bring restoration for those who put their trust in You. Amen.

GOD REMEMBERS
AND FORGIVES

You meet those who gladly do right, those who remember you in your ways. But you were angry, and we sinned; because you hid yourself we transgressed. . . . There is no one who calls on your name, or attempts to take hold of you; for you have hidden your face from us, and have delivered us into the hand of our iniquity. Yet, O LORD, you are our Father; we are the clay, and you are our potter; we are all the work of your hand. Do not be exceedingly angry, O LORD, and do not remember iniquity forever. Now consider, we are all your people.

ISAIAH 64:5, 7–9 NRSV

* How would you describe your relationship with God at this moment? Do you feel like God remembers you or that God is hidden from you?

* As you consider disciplining and correcting your children, how does this passage speak to God's treatment of you as a beloved son who is both disciplined and forgiven?

* Paul often wrote about the tension between God's gracious forgiveness and those who misrepresented him as someone without moral standards. How does this passage speak to that tension between grace and responsibility?

* What is at stake in your choices of obedience and faithfulness today?

- If you've lost sight of God and sinned, what does this passage suggest you should do next?

- How does Isaiah find comfort in being considered the clay shaped by God, who is the potter? If you've read this passage before, how does the idea of fatherhood shape it in particular?

- Isaiah asks that God not remember the sins of Israel forever. How does that request speak to your spiritual experiences right now?

- This passage speaks to both the consequences of disobedience and the mercy of God. How can God's treatment of His people shape how you approach forgiveness and restoration for your children?

Father, I am well aware of my faults and shortcomings. At times I have rejected You and sought my own way rather than listen to Your teachings and direction. Forgive my failures, and give me the discernment to realize when I have abandoned You. Grant the wisdom of Your Spirit so that I can be mindful of You and gladly do what is right. When I fail, restore me with the comfort of Your care for me and lead me forward. Amen.

WHERE TO TAKE BAD NEWS

After Hezekiah received the letter from the messengers and read it, he went up to the LORD's Temple and spread it out before the LORD. And Hezekiah prayed this prayer before the LORD: "O LORD of Heaven's Armies, God of Israel, you are enthroned between the mighty cherubim! You alone are God of all the kingdoms of the earth. You alone created the heavens and the earth. Bend down, O LORD, and listen! Open your eyes, O LORD, and see! Listen to Sennacherib's words of defiance against the living God. It is true, LORD, that the kings of Assyria have destroyed all these nations. . . . Now, O LORD our God, rescue us from his power; then all the kingdoms of the earth will know that you alone, O LORD, are God."

ISAIAH 37:14–18, 20 NLT

+ Hezekiah began his prayer with a kind of reality check that put God in perspective against the kings of the earth. What would your own reality check include if you began your prayer today in the same manner?

+ What is the significance of laying a letter before God? What would it look like for you to spread something that's on your mind before God? When do Christians hold their "letters" back from God, seeking their own solutions or fearing that God won't be able to help them?

+ Part of the reality check in Hezekiah's prayer was to spell out just how deadly and effective the Assyrians had been. How can a kind of naivete or ignorance of a situation make it difficult to pray? What would it look like to fully trust God with a difficult situation?

- Part of the stakes for Hezekiah was the reputation of God and the testimony of God before other nations. Are there ways that your trials or prayers for deliverance can serve as testimonies of God's power at work in your life?

- What is the significance of facing impossible odds in the life of faith? Are there reasons why you may not be willing to face them? How have Christians misunderstood prayers for deliverance at times?

Father, I trust You with my fears, concerns, and doubts today, laying them before You with nothing to hide. I trust in Your concern and in Your power to deliver Your beloved people. May I see both the gravity of my circumstances and the extent of Your abilities to deliver Your people so that I can rest in confidence and hope. Amen.

DON'T LET SHAME STOP YOUR PRAYERS

And I said, "O my God, I am ashamed and embarrassed to lift up my face to You, my God, for our iniquities have risen above our heads and our guilt has grown even to the heavens. Since the days of our fathers to this day we have been in great guilt, and on account of our iniquities we, our kings and our priests have been given into the hand of the kings of the lands, to the sword, to captivity and to plunder and to open shame, as it is this day. But now for a brief moment grace has been shown from the LORD our God, to leave us an escaped remnant and to give us a peg in His holy place, that our God may enlighten our eyes and grant us a little reviving in our bondage."

Ezra 9:6-8 NASB

- ♦ While shame and guilt over sins can make it extremely difficult to approach God in prayer, there was hope even for Israel as they confessed their many sins. When have you felt crushed by your guilt and failures?

- ♦ How have you moved on from failure and shame? In retrospect, how do you think God saw you during that season?

- ♦ Ezra made it clear that although God's people were receiving mercy and forgiveness for their failures, the grace of God was only for a brief moment that could end if they turned away from God again. What do you think is at stake when you confess your sins to God?

- Ezra asked God to enlighten their eyes, trusting God to help the people of Israel move out of their bondage. What would you like to ask God to enlighten in your own life? Are there areas where you need clarity or greater discipline?

- Looking at this passage from the perspective of Christ's death and resurrection, how has God dealt with your guilt and shame? What does that mean for how you pray?

Jesus, You have conquered sin and death, removing the guilt and shame of my life. Enlighten my eyes today so that I can see myself as You see me, and guide me away from whatever continues to hold me back from the freedom You give. May I enter into Your mercy and rest today while You offer it, choosing to live in careful obedience to Your teachings. Amen.

WHERE DO YOU PLACE YOUR HOPE?

*Happy are those whose help is the God of Jacob,
whose hope is in the L<small>ORD</small> their God, who made
heaven and earth, the sea, and all that is in them;
who keeps faith forever; who executes justice for the
oppressed; who gives food to the hungry. The L<small>ORD</small>
sets the prisoners free; the L<small>ORD</small> opens the eyes of
the blind. The L<small>ORD</small> lifts up those who are bowed
down; the L<small>ORD</small> loves the righteous. The L<small>ORD</small> watches
over the strangers; he upholds the orphan and the
widow, but the way of the wicked he brings to ruin.*

P<small>SALM</small> 146:5-9 <small>NRSV</small>

- What are the two paths of life described in today's passage?

- Where do you seek help in times of trouble and difficulty? What are some of the reasons why you may not seek God's help?

- How does society understand happiness, and where is it most common to seek happiness? How does today's psalm suggest you can find happiness?

- How are happiness and hope connected to each other? What can you teach your children about happiness and hope based on this passage?

- When you consider placing your hope in the Lord, what are the types of things this psalm suggests you should keep at the front of your mind? How can those instructions help you remain hopeful?

- Take a moment to consider the list of the kinds of people the Lord helps in this passage. How are these people typically viewed or valued in today's society?

- What can you teach your children about their conduct toward the people listed in this passage?

- What does it look like to be "bowed down" before the Lord? Consider the ways you can live "bowed down" before the Lord so that you can be lifted up.

- As a father, what do you think of the ways the Lord is especially concerned about orphans and widows? What would it look like for you to "uphold" the orphan and widow?

Lord, You want me to place my future and my hope in Your care, and You desire Your children to rely on You and to seek You as their help in the highs and lows of life. Help me to see the people around me who are in need and whose welfare You care about, and may I model Your love and concern for others in front of my children. Help my children to learn to place their hope in You, and may they find happiness in serving others generously. Amen.

ARE YOU PRAYING IN AGREEMENT WITH GOD?

This is what the LORD says: "Be just and fair to all. Do what is right and good, for I am coming soon to rescue you and to display my righteousness among you. Blessed are all those who are careful to do this. Blessed are those who honor my Sabbath days of rest and keep themselves from doing wrong. . . . I will also bless the foreigners who commit themselves to the LORD, who serve him and love his name, who worship him and do not desecrate the Sabbath day of rest, and who hold fast to my covenant. I will bring them to my holy mountain of Jerusalem and will fill them with joy in my house of prayer. I will accept their burnt offerings and sacrifices, because my Temple will be called a house of prayer for all nations."

ISAIAH 56:1-2, 6-7 NLT

♦ God is willing to listen to the prayers of anyone committed to observing His commands. Out of the commands in this passage, which do you find most challenging? Why?

♦ The Sabbath is a vitally important command throughout scripture. Why would God ask His people to put such a high priority on rest? How have you observed or neglected the Sabbath? Are there ways you can grow in observing the Sabbath?

♦ God's desire was for His temple to be a house of prayer. Are there times when prayer is lost in our worship? How can you make your worship experience each week a "house of prayer"?

- Why is God particularly concerned with His people being just and fair in their dealings with others? Are there areas of your life where you can bring greater justice or fairness to others?

- What is the significance of God welcoming foreigners to worship in His temple after the exile and restoration? Are there ways you can become more welcoming to foreigners and exiles?

Lord, You have called me to value justice, fairness, and rest as acts of obedience to Your commands and in accordance with Your covenant promises. May I see the ways my selfishness and pride prompt me to neglect what You care about, and may I welcome those who are rejected or dismissed as outsiders. Today I will seek the rest You offer, and I will take care to examine Your commandments so that they guide my steps throughout my week. Amen.

GOD HONORS PRAYING WITH PERSISTENCE

"I tell you, even though he will not get up and give you the bread because of friendship, yet because of your shameless audacity he will surely get up and give you as much as you need. So I say to you: Ask and it will be given to you; seek and you will find; knock and the door will be opened to you. For everyone who asks receives; the one who seeks finds; and to the one who knocks, the door will be opened. Which of you fathers, if your son asks for a fish, will give him a snake instead? Or if he asks for an egg, will give him a scorpion? If you then, though you are evil, know how to give good gifts to your children, how much more will your Father in heaven give the Holy Spirit to those who ask him!"

Luke 11:8–13 NIV

- What has your experience been asking God for specific requests or making particular needs known in prayer? Have you been more or less likely to share these requests with God in the future?

- How have you responded to prayers that didn't appear to receive an answer from God?

- Trust is a major factor in determining how you pray. Do you believe that God is a loving, caring Father who will treat you like a beloved child, or do you see God as vindictive or abusive? What do you imagine Jesus saying about your views of God the Father?

- Does this story of shamelessly and repeatedly making a prayer request to God encourage or discourage you? Are you more or less likely to pray after reading it?

- There is a risk involved in sharing a prayer request with God, as you will lose control of the results and can't determine how God responds. Is there a prayer that feels particularly risky for you to share today?

- Jesus assured His listeners that the Father gives the Holy Spirit generously to all who ask. How can you become more open to the Spirit's work in your life?

Jesus, You have given me the extraordinary promise that the Father hears my requests and that He will respond. May I pray with confidence in Your promises and with the assurance that the Father seeks my best when I trust myself into His care. Teach me patience and perseverance as I bring my prayer requests to You. Amen.

REMIND YOUR CHILDREN THEY BELONG TO GOD

Remember the days of old; consider the generations long past. Ask your father and he will tell you, your elders, and they will explain to you. When the Most High gave the nations their inheritance, when he divided all mankind, he set up boundaries for the peoples according to the number of the sons of Israel. For the LORD's portion is his people, Jacob his allotted inheritance.

DEUTERONOMY 32:7–9 NIV

+ Why is it so easy to forget the past? What are the implications for your faith if you forget the past?

+ How can remembering God's past faithfulness, as well as your own failures and faithfulness, strengthen your faith and the faith of your children? What is at stake for your children if you don't remind them of what happened in the past?

+ This passage suggests that remembering the past also requires taking initiative, to ask previous generations about God's past actions and faithfulness. Who can you ask from an older generation about God's past faithfulness, especially within your family, church, or community? How could your children benefit from receiving that kind of history?

+ This passage reminded the people of Israel that they belonged in the Promised Land because the Lord had set up its boundaries to include them. How did a sense of belonging in the land help their faith and their future actions?

♦ How can you convey a similar sense of "belonging" or divine provision for your children so that they can have a similar confidence in God?

♦ What do you think it means that the Lord's people are also the Lord's "portion"? How did this statement relate to the faith and actions of the people of Israel? What could it mean for you and your family today?

♦ What is your understanding of an "inheritance" within a family today? How does the concept of an inheritance speak to the kind of faith and security described in today's passage?

♦ How could you explain to your children that they are the Lord's portion or inheritance? What would help them understand and appreciate that possibility?

Father, thank You for the assurance that I am among Your beloved people and inheritance. Help me to live as a member of Your people who have been given blessings and security in You, and may I remind my children of Your deep care for them so that they can live in confidence and hope all the days of their lives. Amen.

NO PROGRESS WITHOUT GOD'S PRESENCE

"Now therefore, I pray You, if I have found favor in Your sight, let me know Your ways that I may know You, so that I may find favor in Your sight. Consider too, that this nation is Your people." And He said, "My presence shall go with you, and I will give you rest." Then he said to Him, "If Your presence does not go with us, do not lead us up from here. For how then can it be known that I have found favor in Your sight, I and Your people? Is it not by Your going with us, so that we, I and Your people, may be distinguished from all the other people who are upon the face of the earth?" . . . Then Moses said, "I pray You, show me Your glory!"

EXODUS 33:13–16, 18 NASB

- The urgency of this prayer from Moses is striking, as he asks God to personally go with the people of Israel. He wouldn't even go without God's presence. What are you facing today for which you have a desperate need for God's presence?

- When you face a particularly difficult challenge, you also have an opportunity to draw near to God and to see God's power at work. How have you seen God work on your behalf in the past?

- Moses actively interceded for the people of Israel after they had sinned and departed from the Lord. Is there a situation where you can intercede for others in prayer?

- Why do people neglect to intercede with God on behalf of others? Are there reasons why you may be hesitant to intercede for someone else?

- Given an opportunity to make a direct request of God, Moses asked for God to reveal His glory to him. Why do you think Moses made this request when he had such intimate access with God already?

- How was Moses different after experiencing God's glory? In what ways have you experienced God so that you were changed?

Lord, You desire to reveal Yourself to me, and You are attentive to prayers on behalf of others. Open my eyes to the needs of others, and grant me the wisdom and courage to pray with truth and compassion on behalf of those who are in need of You. May my life bear the marks of Your loving presence so that I am transformed and more aware of others. Amen.

REMEMBER AND CELEBRATE GOD'S WORKS

Make a joyful noise to God, all the earth; sing the glory of his name; give to him glorious praise. Say to God, "How awesome are your deeds! Because of your great power, your enemies cringe before you. All the earth worships you; they sing praises to you, sing praises to your name." Come and see what God has done: he is awesome in his deeds among mortals. He turned the sea into dry land; they passed through the river on foot. There we rejoiced in him, who rules by his might forever, whose eyes keep watch on the nations—let the rebellious not exalt themselves. Bless our God, O peoples, let the sound of his praise be heard, who has kept us among the living, and has not let our feet slip.

PSALM 66:1–9 NRSV

- ◆ Worship serves as an important part of remembering what God has done and His power over the world. How have you remembered what God has done in your life? Has a particular song proven meaningful to you?

- ◆ Is there something that you need to surrender to God or depend on Him to address? How has God acted in the past when you have relied on Him?

- ◆ The Bible makes a practice of retelling stories to remember God's deliverance and to celebrate God's power. Is there a story that you have come to rely on as an example of God's presence in your life that gives you greater faith?

- How does celebration impact your faith? Do you find yourself praying differently when you remember God's past deliverance and mercy?

- This psalm invites others to see God's works. How does God's work in your life become something that concerns others?

- When God's power is seen in perspective, you have a potent reminder of the consequences of rejecting God or living in disobedience. Why is this perspective so vital for prayer?

Lord, Your power was on display for Your people and the surrounding nations when You delivered them from the powerful army of Egypt and guided them into the Promised Land. Even today You desire to reveal Your strength and mercy to me, delivering me from evil so that I can testify to Your faithfulness. May my words and worship today call to mind Your saving help so that my faith grows and my prayers are supported by the memory of Your deliverance. Amen.

WE PRAY WITH CONFIDENCE IN GOD'S LOVE

We know how much God loves us, and we have put our trust in his love. God is love, and all who live in love live in God, and God lives in them. And as we live in God, our love grows more perfect. So we will not be afraid on the day of judgment, but we can face him with confidence because we live like Jesus here in this world. Such love has no fear, because perfect love expels all fear. If we are afraid, it is for fear of punishment, and this shows that we have not fully experienced his perfect love. We love each other because he loved us first.

1 JOHN 4:16–19 NLT

- John took confidence in God's love. Are you aware of God's love for you? Is this something that you can truly trust in as you begin to pray today?

- What does it mean to you that "God is love"? Have Christians that you know sometimes portrayed God as being primarily concerned with something other than love?

- God's desire is to be united with His people, and love is one of the ways that God's love draws His people closer to one another. What does it look like for you to "live in love"?

- Growing deeper in God's love gives confidence for the Day of Judgment because of God's transforming power. How have you seen God at work in your life?

Are there ways you can make more space to connect with God's love?

- Fear is the opposite of the security of God's love. If you have struggles with fear, especially fear of God that goes beyond a healthy respect for Him, then you may consider meditating on God's love as you pray today. How can you experience God's perfect love?

- God does not demand our love without first becoming vulnerable and reaching out to us in love. What is your reaction to God's desire to love you in this way?

Father, You have reached out to me with Your perfect love, and You promise to drive out my fears and uncertainties. Open my mind to the depth of Your love for me, and drive away my fears with the security You give. May my life become united with Your love so that Your love grows, takes root in my life, and transforms how I treat others. Amen.

SERVE WITH
CHILDLIKE DEVOTION

But I hope in the Lord Jesus to send Timothy to you shortly, so that I also may be encouraged when I learn of your condition. For I have no one else of kindred spirit who will genuinely be concerned for your welfare. For they all seek after their own interests, not those of Christ Jesus. But you know of his proven worth, that he served with me in the furtherance of the gospel like a child serving his father. Therefore I hope to send him immediately, as soon as I see how things go with me; and I trust in the Lord that I myself also will be coming shortly.

PHILIPPIANS 2:19-24 NASB

* What made Timothy so valuable for ministry in the eyes of Paul? In what ways did Timothy distinguish himself from others serving in ministry?

* Do you and the people in your church value the same kinds of qualities for leaders and volunteers in ministry today? What gets in the way of the kind of service that Timothy modeled?

* What does it look like to seek after the interests of Christ Jesus rather than your own interests? How can you model that kind of service for your children?

* What would be involved in ministry that is the "furtherance of the Gospel"? Do you recall any clues from other passages of scripture, such as the book of Acts, that describe Timothy's ministry?

- Why would Paul compare Timothy's service and devotion to a child serving his father? What kinds of words would you use to describe that kind of devotion?

- What gets in the way of serving others with childlike devotion and concern for their interests alone?

- What does it look like to have proven character? In what kinds of situations can you model this kind of character for your children?

- What did Paul have to lose in sending Timothy to the Philippians? Why would he take that risk anyway?

Jesus, thank You for the model of Timothy so that I can aspire to regard and to serve others with his same commitment and concern. May humility and a desire to please You alone guide my choices so that I never place myself first. Help me to value leaders who model exemplary character and genuine love for others, and may I put Your concerns above my own when I lead and serve others. Amen.

PRAY FOR AN UNCERTAIN FUTURE

"Be careful, or your hearts will be weighed down with carousing, drunkenness and the anxieties of life, and that day will close on you suddenly like a trap. For it will come on all those who live on the face of the whole earth. Be always on the watch, and pray that you may be able to escape all that is about to happen, and that you may be able to stand before the Son of Man." Each day Jesus was teaching at the temple, and each evening he went out to spend the night on the hill called the Mount of Olives, and all the people came early in the morning to hear him at the temple.

LUKE 21:34-38 NIV

- ◆ God will one day bring our secrets to light, so Jesus teaches us to drop our pretenses and to confess our sins today. How does the idea of a trap in this passage speak to you?

- ◆ Some of the signs of a heart that is far from God include an absorption with the pursuit of pleasure or an obsession with the anxieties of life. When have you noticed these signs in your life?

- ◆ While Jesus assured His followers that no one knows the day or the hour of His return, how does an awareness of His return direct your attention and priorities?

- What does it mean for you to be on "watch" for the return of Jesus? Is this a frightened, worried posture, or is there a positive element to this watchfulness?

- The people of Jerusalem faced the frightening prospect of their city being attacked, but Jesus encouraged them to pray that they would escape. How has God's compassion and mercy been manifested in challenging or dangerous situations in your life?

- Jesus left the temple each evening to spend time in solitude on the Mount of Olives, presumably to pray. How do you think solitude impacted the way He taught others? Are there opportunities for you to explore solitude today?

Jesus, You desire to save me from calamity, from the sting of regret, and from the day of judgment when my actions will be called to account. May I remain watchful over my actions today and aware that Your return could be at any moment. As I seek You today, whether in solitude or in a city, may I find the satisfaction and peace of Your presence that delivers me from the cares of this world and the anxieties of life. Amen.

ADDRESS WORRY
WITH PRAYER

Rejoice in the Lord always; again I will say, Rejoice. Let your gentleness be known to everyone. The Lord is near. Do not worry about anything, but in everything by prayer and supplication with thanksgiving let your requests be made known to God. And the peace of God, which surpasses all understanding, will guard your hearts and your minds in Christ Jesus. Finally, beloved, whatever is true, whatever is honorable, whatever is just, whatever is pure, whatever is pleasing, whatever is commendable, if there is any excellence and if there is anything worthy of praise, think about these things. Keep on doing the things that you have learned and received and heard and seen in me, and the God of peace will be with you.

PHILIPPIANS 4:4–9 NRSV

- While Paul said that you should rejoice in the Lord always, are there times when you have not been inclined to rejoice?

- Have you seen benefits to rejoicing in situations when it was the last thing on your mind?

- Worry is a natural and understandable response to challenges or stress in life, but Paul offered a simple response for worry: pray. What are you worried about today? Beginning with thanksgiving, share your concerns with God.

- Have you experienced the peace that "surpasses all understanding" in your life? If not, why do you think this peace has been elusive for you? If you have, how did you arrive at that point?

- The peace that God gives comes when you surrender your concerns to Him, but the nature of this peace remains a mystery. What do you make of this mystery?

- Experiencing God's peace is also linked to training your mind to return to holy, pure topics. What kinds of things would you consider true, honorable, just, pure, or praiseworthy?

- Obedience is considered essential for prayer and experiencing the peace of God. What do you recall from Paul's ministry that is worthy of imitation?

Jesus, You promise to alleviate my worries and to grant Your peace if I commit myself to making my requests known to You. May Your Spirit call to mind the hidden cares or the obscured distractions that prevent me from fully opening myself up to You. As I go about my day, direct my thinking to truthful, encouraging thoughts so that I can remain blameless before You and pray with confidence in Your redeeming power. Amen.

BOLDLY ASKING FOR GOD'S BLESSING

"Now therefore, O Lord God, the word that You have spoken concerning Your servant and his house, confirm it forever, and do as You have spoken, that Your name may be magnified forever, by saying, 'The Lord of hosts is God over Israel'; and may the house of Your servant David be established before You. For You, O Lord of hosts, the God of Israel, have made a revelation to Your servant, saying, 'I will build you a house'; therefore Your servant has found courage to pray this prayer to You. Now, O Lord God, You are God, and Your words are truth, and You have promised this good thing to Your servant. Now therefore, may it please You to bless the house of Your servant, that it may continue forever before You. For You, O Lord God, have spoken; and with Your blessing may the house of Your servant be blessed forever."

2 Samuel 7:25-29 nasb

- Perhaps God has spoken in your life, but is there a reason to ask God for confirmation? Why do you think David asked for confirmation?

- Are there blessings you have received that could serve as a sign of God's power in your life or as an encouragement for others?

- At a time when God had been blessing David richly, he boldly asked God for even greater blessings. Are there opportunities for you to ask God for more or to stretch your faith in greater ways?

- How did David see his own fate tied in with God's reputation? How could God be glorified in your life based on what He has revealed to you in prayer?

- David asked God boldly for His blessing because he knew that God delighted in doing so. Is there any reason for you to doubt God's pleasure in responding to your prayer requests?

Lord, You delight in blessing Your people and revealing Yourself to them. I ask that You remain attentive to my requests and guide me toward security in You and Your promises. Bring Your promises and blessings to pass, and guard me from temptation or any desire that would draw me away from Your will being done. I ask for the renewal of Your mercies this morning and the boldness to rest in Your promises. May Your name be glorified in my life today. Amen.

WE PRAY FOR GOD'S STRENGTH IN OTHERS

For now we really live, since you are standing firm in the Lord. How can we thank God enough for you in return for all the joy we have in the presence of our God because of you? Night and day we pray most earnestly that we may see you again and supply what is lacking in your faith. Now may our God and Father himself and our Lord Jesus clear the way for us to come to you. May the Lord make your love increase and overflow for each other and for everyone else, just as ours does for you. May he strengthen your hearts so that you will be blameless and holy in the presence of our God and Father when our Lord Jesus comes with all his holy ones.

1 Thessalonians 3:8–13 NIV

- A significant portion of Paul's prayers were concerned with the faith of the churches he had planted and whether these new believers were standing firm in the Lord. Is there someone you can pray for today, perhaps someone who is on shaky ground in their faith?

- Where do people typically expect to find joy? Is it surprising to you that Paul found his joy in the faith of the church he planted? How can you make investments in others so that your joy will be more directly tied to God's life in others?

- Is there something that you have prayed about night and day? Do you believe this kind of urgent prayer could be a more regular part of your life, or do you see it as an occasional time of intercession?

- In his prayers, Paul laid out his desire to visit this church, but obstacles remained that he asked God to clear. Is there an obstacle blocking your way today? What is keeping you from where you believe you need to go, and how can you trust this obstacle to God in prayer?

Jesus, You desire to use me to strengthen Your Church and to bless others, and You hear my prayer requests and intercessions for others. May I turn my eyes away from my own needs, concerns, and plans so that I can see the ways that the people around me need to know You or grow deeper in their love for You. May my prayers become a support and a ministry to them so that we may share the joy of Your life and love together. Amen.

ARE WE WILLING TO LEARN FROM GOD?

It is for discipline that you endure; God deals with you as with sons; for what son is there whom his father does not discipline? But if you are without discipline, of which all have become partakers, then you are illegitimate children and not sons. Furthermore, we had earthly fathers to discipline us, and we respected them; shall we not much rather be subject to the Father of spirits, and live? For they disciplined us for a short time as seemed best to them, but He disciplines us for our good, so that we may share His holiness. All discipline for the moment seems not to be joyful, but sorrowful; yet to those who have been trained by it, afterwards it yields the peaceful fruit of righteousness.

HEBREWS 12:7-11 NASB

- What is the difference between constructive, life-giving discipline and destructive and discouraging discipline?

- What has been your experience with discipline as both a son and as a father? What may be different when you consider God's approach to discipline?

- Ponder for a moment what discipline from God could look like. Can you name a situation or two where you believe God was disciplining you?

- The author of Hebrews describes God's discipline as a positive, encouraging sign that God regards you as a son. What has been your reaction to God's discipline? How does this passage speak to that?

- Discipline is described as a temporary process that has a specific goal. How does that help you think about God's discipline for you?

- What is the payoff for enduring discipline?

- What could you apply from God's approach to discipline to your own parenting and discipline of your children?

- How can you help your children see discipline as a positive process for them?

Father, thank You for treating me as a beloved son and caring enough about me to guide my steps with Your discipline. Help me to see the ways You are directing my steps so that I can fully share in Your holiness and peace. May I have the wisdom and perseverance to see how You are disciplining and guiding me so that I can trust in Your love and care. Help me to train my children in the same way, with care and love, so that they learn the right ways to live and so they are always mindful of Your love and concern. Amen.

GOD SEES OUR HEARTS

*This is what the L*ord *says: "Heaven is my throne,
and the earth is my footstool. Could you build me a
temple as good as that? Could you build me such
a resting place? My hands have made both heaven
and earth; they and everything in them are mine. I,
the L*ord*, have spoken! I will bless those who have
humble and contrite hearts, who tremble at my word.
But those who choose their own ways—delighting
in their detestable sins—will not have their offerings
accepted. When such people sacrifice a bull, it is no
more acceptable than a human sacrifice. When they
sacrifice a lamb, it's as though they had sacrificed
a dog! When they bring an offering of grain, they
might as well offer the blood of a pig. When they burn
frankincense, it's as if they had blessed an idol."*

Isaiah 66:1–3 nlt

- ◆ Have there been times when you tried to do great
  things for God but lost touch with God personally?
  Did you find that you were more or less likely to pray
  during those times?

- ◆ How does the image of God sitting on a throne above
  the earth speak to the way you think of God today
  and how you pray? Are there reasons why you may
  struggle to believe in God's power and authority in
  the world?

- ◆ While God's people had become focused on the
  place where they worshipped God, the Lord turned

their eyes to the splendor of creation and what He desires from His people—humble, contrite hearts. What are the distractions that have kept you from seeing God's work in this world?

- Are there reasons why humility and contrition have been struggles for God's people? Where are you today when it comes to humility before God?

- God is more concerned with the state of your heart than with the specifics of your religious observance. How can you keep God's words close to your heart so that your acts of worship are meaningful this week?

Lord, may my prayers rise to You out of a deep awareness of Your glory, awe for Your power, and reverence for Your commands that give life. May my heart remain fully committed to You so that all my actions flow from a desire to remain close to You. May my joy become complete as I celebrate You and Your love today. Amen.

THANK GOD FOR HIS CHURCH

I thank my God every time I remember you. In all my prayers for all of you, I always pray with joy because of your partnership in the gospel from the first day until now, being confident of this, that he who began a good work in you will carry it on to completion until the day of Christ Jesus. . . . And this is my prayer: that your love may abound more and more in knowledge and depth of insight, so that you may be able to discern what is best and may be pure and blameless for the day of Christ, filled with the fruit of righteousness that comes through Jesus Christ—to the glory and praise of God.

PHILIPPIANS 1:3-6, 9-11 NIV

+ The joyful fellowship of believers is a gift from God as He sustains His Church and joins them together as the body of Christ. Are there fellow Christians you are particularly thankful for today?

+ Is there someone you know who has started to experience the gifts of God but has not yet seen them come to completion? Consider how you can intercede for this person to grow into this completion.

+ Paul's confidence for his fellow believers grew out of his hope in the Lord and the Lord's commitment to His people. Take a moment to meditate on how God will complete His good works in your life. How does this speak to you today?

+ What does it mean for the love of these believers to grow in knowledge and depth of insight? How have you seen God's love grow in your life? Is this something you can request to see grow in the weeks to come?

- How does your growth in love impact your discernment and purity?

- As you pray, consider Paul's words that his readers would be filled with the fruit of righteousness that comes through Jesus Christ. Have you been relying on your own efforts to grow spiritually or to become righteous? How can Jesus help you today?

Jesus, You have begun a good work in me, and I trust that You are able to complete it. May Your love take root and grow in me as I look to You as my source of life and strength. May I grow in discernment and wisdom so that I can determine what is right and live in obedience to You. I ask for these things based on Your mercy and love. Amen.

PRAY FOR ENEMIES AND OPPONENTS

This is what the LORD of Heaven's Armies, the God of Israel, says to all the captives he has exiled to Babylon from Jerusalem: "Build homes, and plan to stay. Plant gardens, and eat the food they produce. Marry and have children. Then find spouses for them so that you may have many grandchildren. Multiply! Do not dwindle away! And work for the peace and prosperity of the city where I sent you into exile. Pray to the LORD for it, for its welfare will determine your welfare." This is what the LORD of Heaven's Armies, the God of Israel, says: "Do not let your prophets and fortune-tellers who are with you in the land of Babylon trick you. Do not listen to their dreams, because they are telling you lies in my name. I have not sent them," says the LORD.

JEREMIAH 29:4–9 NLT

- Jeremiah told the people of Israel that they were supposed to not only pray for their enemies but work for their prosperity. How have you responded to an enemy or opponent? What would it look like to pray for that person's prosperity and peace?

- The welfare of Israel depended on the welfare of their city. How can you grow in awareness of your own city and work for its benefit? Are there people in your city who need your prayers today?

- Even in a time of loss and disorientation in exile, the people of Israel were encouraged to marry, have children, and work hard in a foreign land. How has God guided you through difficult or disorienting times? How is God guiding you to hope for the future?

- It's easy to look for the people who will tell us what we want to hear rather than listening for what God is truly telling us. Are there times when you have struggled to discern God's voice?

- How do you discern when a message in scripture or the direction you receive in prayer is coming from God?

Father, You walk with Your children through their difficulties and remain with them after they suffer the consequences of their sins. Help me to stay close to You and aware of Your direction for my life. May I place my hope in Your promises and work toward the prosperity of my city, the benefit of my neighbors, and the restoration of my enemies. May I continue to follow Your direction even when others suggest an easier, more appealing path. Amen.

JESUS WANTS US TO PRAY FOR EVERYONE

I urge, then, first of all, that petitions, prayers, intercession and thanksgiving be made for all people—for kings and all those in authority, that we may live peaceful and quiet lives in all godliness and holiness. This is good, and pleases God our Savior, who wants all people to be saved and to come to a knowledge of the truth. For there is one God and one mediator between God and mankind, the man Christ Jesus, who gave himself as a ransom for all people. This has now been witnessed to at the proper time. And for this purpose I was appointed a herald and an apostle—I am telling the truth, I am not lying— and a true and faithful teacher of the Gentiles.

1 TIMOTHY 2:1-7 NIV

- Paul urged his readers to commit to praying for all people with all kinds of prayers: petitions, intercessions, and thanksgiving. What roles do these kinds of prayers play in the Christian life?

- Of the prayers listed above, do you find yourself drawn to one kind of prayer? Why? Is there a kind of prayer that you need to grow or put into practice on a more regular basis?

- Although Paul suffered a great deal at the hands of rulers and those in authority, he remained committed to praying for them. What are the reasons he stated for these prayers? Is there a local authority you can commit to pray for today?

- If there is peace in the world, the Gospel is free to advance without the threat of war keeping people from its message. How can you contribute to the promotion of peace in the world? How are your prayers for the spreading of the Gospel linked to praying for peace?

- What does it mean for you that Jesus is the mediator between God and man? Why do some fear Jesus instead of relying on Him as their advocate and mediator?

Jesus, You offered Your life to save me because of Your great compassion for me and because You hope to save all people from sin and death. May I come to You in prayer today with confidence in Your mercy and salvation so that I can rest in Your present love and so that I can make prayer requests for the benefit of others. I ask for peace and stability among our leaders and justice for all people. Amen.

THE POWER OF PRAYING FOR ACCUSERS

*"Now therefore, take for yourselves seven bulls
and seven rams, and go to My servant Job, and
offer up a burnt offering for yourselves, and My
servant Job will pray for you. For I will accept him
so that I may not do with you according to your
folly, because you have not spoken of Me what
is right, as My servant Job has." So Eliphaz the
Temanite and Bildad the Shuhite and Zophar the
Naamathite went and did as the LORD told them;
and the LORD accepted Job. The LORD restored
the fortunes of Job when he prayed for his friends,
and the LORD increased all that Job had twofold.*

JOB 42:8–10 NASB

♦ Imagine for a moment that you are a friend of Job
who had accused him of sin. How would you respond
to God's rebuke of your beliefs? What would it feel
like for Job to pray for you?

♦ Was there a time when you believed something
that you found out later to be wrong? How did you
address that wrong and then move on with your
beliefs?

♦ What does this story teach you about facing conflict
with others? How does prayer help you become
reconciled with others?

♦ When Job's friends learned of their error, they
humbled themselves and followed God's commands.
How does this story guide you in repentance?

- Job had every reason to abandon his friends after they failed to comfort him and accused him of sinning against God. However, his prayer for them brought them healing and restored his prosperity. Is there someone who has wronged you that you can pray for today?

- While Job did experience prosperity again, he had already suffered a great deal. How does the conclusion of his story appear to you? How do you think Job interacted with his wealth and position after suffering so much?

- Job's story doesn't offer a tidy answer to the reason for suffering in the world. How has the problem of pain and suffering impacted the way you pray?

Father, You have compassion on me and remain present with me in the midst of my suffering and pain. Guide me away from bitterness and unforgiveness so that I can freely become reconciled with others. When I have wronged others, may I remember Your mercy and confess my sins with confidence in Your restoration. I trust You today with my well-being and with the events that are yet to take place. Amen.

WHERE IS YOUR
HEART TURNING?

*"But for you who fear my name, the Sun of
Righteousness will rise with healing in his wings.
And you will go free, leaping with joy like calves
let out to pasture. On the day when I act, you will
tread upon the wicked as if they were dust under
your feet," says the LORD of Heaven's Armies.
"Remember to obey the Law of Moses, my servant—
all the decrees and regulations that I gave him on
Mount Sinai for all Israel. Look, I am sending you
the prophet Elijah before the great and dreadful
day of the LORD arrives. His preaching will turn
the hearts of fathers to their children, and the
hearts of children to their fathers. Otherwise I
will come and strike the land with a curse."*

MALACHI 4:2–6 NLT

• How would you describe the type of person who
  does not fear God's name? What kinds of choices
  does that person make?

• What does it look like for you to fear God's name?
  What are some other words that you could use to
  convey this type of "fear"?

• Ponder what it looks like for you to enjoy the benefits
  of fearing God's name and living in obedience to God.

- Whether in a relationship with God or in a parent/child relationship, how can fear undermine the connection with each other?

- The expression "turning your heart" toward someone is an important image in this passage. What do you think it means here?

- Take a moment to consider where your heart is directed right now. Is your heart turned toward God and your children, or is there another direction that your heart is turned toward right now?

- What difference does it make for Israel to remember the "decrees and regulations" that were given on Mount Sinai? What is the significance of this kind of obedience in your life?

- This passage says a lot about obeying God's commands, but it also says that children and fathers will have their hearts turned to each other. Why is it important to address the direction of their hearts? What is the significance of them turning to each other in particular?

Father, You are compassionate and promise freedom to Your people, but You also hold me accountable for my disobedience. May I never take Your mercy and promises for granted, and may I always keep my children on my heart so that I can love, teach, and cherish them all the days of my life. Amen.

DEVELOP DAILY DEVOTION TO PRAYER

Devote yourselves to prayer with an alert mind and a thankful heart. Pray for us, too, that God will give us many opportunities to speak about his mysterious plan concerning Christ. That is why I am here in chains. Pray that I will proclaim this message as clearly as I should. Live wisely among those who are not believers, and make the most of every opportunity. . . . Epaphras, a member of your own fellowship and a servant of Christ Jesus, sends you his greetings. He always prays earnestly for you, asking God to make you strong and perfect, fully confident that you are following the whole will of God. I can assure you that he prays hard for you and also for the believers in Laodicea and Hierapolis.

COLOSSIANS 4:2-5, 12-13 NLT

- The centerpiece of Christian living for Paul as he ended his letters was prayer. He encouraged his readers to devote themselves to prayer. What would devotion to prayer look like for you this week?

- While we often enter into prayer with a thankful heart, what does it look like to pray with an alert mind? How would you describe the state of your mind when you have prayed lately?

- Paul asked for his churches to pray for him because he relied on their prayers to accomplish his ministry. How can you pray for the leaders in your church or in your circles today?

- It's understandable to wonder what God has planned in a time of suffering, such as Paul's time in prison. How have you sought God in times of difficulty or suffering?

- Is there a particular prayer request that you are praying about earnestly and often? How have you approached such an urgent request?

- Part of prayer is trusting God to work in others for their benefit. How can you let go of something today and trust God to bring it to completion?

Jesus, I thank You for the gift of Your Holy Spirit and the comfort of Your promises to remain with Your people in times of difficulty and suffering. May I speak clearly and boldly of Your love and take every opportunity possible to share it with those who need it. Give me the wisdom to support those who minister and to notice the ways You are at work in those around me. In Your strength and by Your mercy, I will remain faithful to Your calling for my life. Amen.

PRAY IN SECRET BEFORE GOD

"Be careful not to practice your righteousness in front of others to be seen by them. If you do, you will have no reward from your Father in heaven. . . . And when you pray, do not be like the hypocrites, for they love to pray standing in the synagogues and on the street corners to be seen by others. Truly I tell you, they have received their reward in full. But when you pray, go into your room, close the door and pray to your Father, who is unseen. Then your Father, who sees what is done in secret, will reward you. And when you pray, do not keep on babbling like pagans, for they think they will be heard because of their many words. Do not be like them, for your Father knows what you need before you ask him."

MATTHEW 6:1, 5-8 NIV

- Jesus warned that pious acts and praying to get noticed will deprive you of your reward from God the Father. What does it mean to you that God rewards His people for their actions?

- Jesus noted that hypocrites pray in public spaces in order to be noticed while they pray. What does it look like to pray in sincerity and good faith in a public worship setting or in church?

- Why would someone pray publicly in order to be noticed? How have you dealt with this temptation?

- Have you made a point of praying in solitude, "clos[ing] the door" of your room when seeking God? How has solitude impacted the way you pray?

- Many teachers of prayer throughout the history of the Church have interpreted verse 6 figuratively, seeing the inner room as an invitation to pray privately with God in your heart. How does this interpretation speak to you?

- How does it impact the way you pray if you realize that God already knows what you need before you make a request for it? Why is it still important to make your needs known to God even if God already knows about them?

Father, I will seek You today with the confidence that You know my needs and that You desire to care for me, meeting my needs based on Your mercy and grace. I trust that You delight in hearing from Your people and that You are not interested in our words or techniques but are looking at the sincerity of our hearts. Amen.

JESUS RELATES TO OUR SUFFERING AND SUPPLICATION

For every high priest taken from among men is appointed on behalf of men in things pertaining to God, in order to offer both gifts and sacrifices for sins; he can deal gently with the ignorant and misguided, since he himself also is beset with weakness. . . . In the days of His flesh, He offered up both prayers and supplications with loud crying and tears to the One able to save Him from death, and He was heard because of His piety. Although He was a Son, He learned obedience from the things which He suffered. And having been made perfect, He became to all those who obey Him the source of eternal salvation, being designated by God as a high priest according to the order of Melchizedek.

HEBREWS 5:1-2, 7-10 NASB

- While the words *high priest* may give the impression that a priest is somehow removed from your everyday needs, what is the designated function of a high priest? How does this connect to the way you can relate to God through Jesus?

- If you are struggling spiritually or lack knowledge of God, how can Jesus minister to you as the High Priest?

- What does it mean that Jesus bore your same weaknesses? After considering this truth, in what ways are you able to pray differently when you recall how deeply Jesus can relate to your struggles?

- Obedience to God can come through suffering, teaching dependence on God when there is so much at stake. How has suffering changed you? Do you pray differently during a difficult season of life?

- While Jesus continued to be fully God while on earth, He still cried out to God and made His needs known to God on a regular basis. If Jesus depended so much on prayer despite being one with God, what does this mean for how you approach prayer?

Jesus, You bore the same weaknesses, desires, and suffering that I endure on this earth. Teach me to rely on the Spirit's help, to continually seek You in prayer, and to learn obedience through my suffering. May I never forget that You are a sympathetic high priest who desires to meet me in my weaknesses so that You can show mercy, intercede on my behalf, and guide me to the way of life. Hear my cries to You as I live in obedience and holiness, following Your commands. Amen.

WAIT ON THE LORD, HOPE IN HIM

The faithful love of the LORD never ends! His mercies never cease. Great is his faithfulness; his mercies begin afresh each morning. I say to myself, "The LORD is my inheritance; therefore, I will hope in him!" The LORD is good to those who depend on him, to those who search for him. So it is good to wait quietly for salvation from the LORD. And it is good for people to submit at an early age to the yoke of his discipline: let them sit alone in silence beneath the LORD's demands. Let them lie face down in the dust, for there may be hope at last. Let them turn the other cheek to those who strike them and accept the insults of their enemies. For no one is abandoned by the Lord forever. Though he brings grief, he also shows compassion because of the greatness of his unfailing love.

LAMENTATIONS 3:22–32 NLT

- Although people may falter in their loyalty to God, the love of God for His people is steadfast and endures. Have you ever believed that God's mercy for you has run out? How has that impacted the way you pray?

- What would it mean for you to begin each day by claiming the promise of God's new mercies for you?

- Consider the idea of the Lord becoming your inheritance. What kinds of investments would you expect to make to ensure that the Lord is your inheritance?

- What are you relying on God to do for you or how are you relying on God to guide you today? Are you waiting on God or searching for God in any particular way?

- Why is waiting in silence so important for Christians? When you have waited for God to act, was it difficult to remain silent? How might silence before God help you grow in your faith?

- Accepting insults and injuries from others can be degrading and difficult. What is God teaching you through suffering quietly through those challenges?

- God's love never fails, but when have you doubted this? How have you held on to the promises of God when circumstances appeared hopeless?

Lord, I trust in Your unfailing love and new mercies today, waiting in patience for You to guide me. Your compassion and love will guide me through times of uncertainty and failure, and I will wait on Your rescue in silence. Amen.

PATIENTLY WAIT FOR THE LORD

Dear brothers and sisters, be patient as you wait for the Lord's return. Consider the farmers who patiently wait for the rains in the fall and in the spring. They eagerly look for the valuable harvest to ripen. You, too, must be patient. Take courage, for the coming of the Lord is near. Don't grumble about each other, brothers and sisters, or you will be judged. For look—the Judge is standing at the door! For examples of patience in suffering, dear brothers and sisters, look at the prophets who spoke in the name of the Lord. We give great honor to those who endure under suffering. For instance, you know about Job, a man of great endurance. You can see how the Lord was kind to him at the end, for the Lord is full of tenderness and mercy.

JAMES 5:7-11 NLT

+ While it may seem that the wicked are prospering and your prayers are not effective, James assured his readers that they should patiently wait for the Lord's return. How does waiting for the Lord's return impact the way you pray?

+ What do farmers reveal to you about waiting for growth and the coming of an abundant harvest? Back in James's time, how much control did farmers have over the growth of their crops?

+ Why was James particularly concerned about Christians grumbling against one another? Why do you think divisions with fellow Christians can be particularly harmful for your faith?

- What are some of the reasons James encouraged his readers to endure suffering? What has helped you endure hardships and suffering?

- How does the image of the Lord standing at the door, as if He is a judge about to enter the room, impact how you think of prayer and obedience today?

- What does the story of Job teach you about God's mercy in the midst of hardship? Are there times that you may hesitate to compare your story to Job's?

Lord, grant me the patience to wait for You and the humility to live at peace with fellow believers. I trust in Your tenderness and mercy as I go through hardships and uncertainties, believing that the ways You have provided for others will also come to fruition for me. May I find courage in the strength You provide, and may You find me faithful and unashamed when I stand before You. Amen.

PRAYER ENDURES
FOR GENERATIONS

*But you, O LORD, are enthroned forever; your name
endures to all generations. You will rise up and
have compassion on Zion, for it is time to favor it;
the appointed time has come. For your servants
hold its stones dear, and have pity on its dust.
The nations will fear the name of the LORD, and
all the kings of the earth your glory. For the LORD
will build up Zion; he will appear in his glory. He
will regard the prayer of the destitute, and will
not despise their prayer. Let this be recorded for a
generation to come, so that a people yet unborn
may praise the LORD: that he looked down from
his holy height, from heaven the LORD looked at
the earth, to hear the groans of the prisoners,
to set free those who were doomed to die.*

PSALM 102:12-20 NRSV

* When everything else in your life appears uncertain or in chaos, the Lord remains certain. How can you take comfort in the stability of God in a difficult time?

* Is it possible that sometimes we pray as if God is fragile or will not be able to handle the scale of our problems? How does this psalm address that concern?

* In a season of loss, it's possible to fear being forgotten by God or to worry that your prayers are being ignored. How does this psalm grapple with that concern?

- There is a larger view of faithfulness in this psalm where the prayers of God's people have an impact on future generations. Who are the people who will follow you that you feel led to pray for today?

- God takes pity on those who are trapped or who long for freedom. How can you share God's compassion for those who have lost hope? Are there ways you can reach out to people who can't figure out a path forward?

Lord, my prayers today aren't just for my benefit but for the benefit of those who follow me. May Your love take root in my life so that I can share Your abundance with others. Even when my future is in jeopardy, I will find my hope in You, trusting that You have not turned Your back on Your chosen people. May those who have lost hope find restoration and peace, and may those who follow me learn of Your faithfulness. Amen.

HOW GOD HELPS US PRAY

We know that the whole creation has been groaning as in the pains of childbirth right up to the present time. Not only so, but we ourselves, who have the firstfruits of the Spirit, groan inwardly as we wait eagerly for our adoption to sonship, the redemption of our bodies. For in this hope we were saved. But hope that is seen is no hope at all. Who hopes for what they already have? But if we hope for what we do not yet have, we wait for it patiently. In the same way, the Spirit helps us in our weakness. We do not know what we ought to pray for, but the Spirit himself intercedes for us through wordless groans. And he who searches our hearts knows the mind of the Spirit, because the Spirit intercedes for God's people in accordance with the will of God.

ROMANS 8:22–27 NIV

- Do you believe you have been given the Holy Spirit from God as the firstfruits of God's blessing for you? Take time to meditate on the nature of the Spirit's gift for you.

- The groans of the Spirit and of creation for the redemption of our world suggest that all is not as God intends. Is there something that isn't as God intends in your life or relationships that you can join God in praying for today?

- What does it mean for you to be adopted as God's son? What makes it difficult to remember that blessing most days?

- Hope that is seen is not "hope," because it must be something unseen and anticipated. What are you hoping for today? Are there things that God is calling you to hope for in this season of your life?

- God is not surprised by your weaknesses, and the Holy Spirit is present to guide you in how to pray despite your weaknesses. Is there a particular weakness that you would like to confess to God?

- While the Spirit searches your mind and heart in order to intercede for you, how can you partner with the Spirit's work in your life?

Jesus, You sent Your Holy Spirit to save me from my weaknesses and errors. I trust that You are present in my life through the Spirit's work and that the Spirit will advocate for me and guide me in the way I should pray. May I move toward Your will under the Spirit's direction and wisdom. Amen.

ARE YOU WILLING TO LEARN?

Therefore let all the faithful pray to you while you may be found; surely the rising of the mighty waters will not reach them. You are my hiding place; you will protect me from trouble and surround me with songs of deliverance. I will instruct you and teach you in the way you should go; I will counsel you with my loving eye on you. Do not be like the horse or the mule, which have no understanding but must be controlled by bit and bridle or they will not come to you. Many are the woes of the wicked, but the LORD's unfailing love surrounds the one who trusts in him. Rejoice in the LORD and be glad, you righteous; sing, all you who are upright in heart!

PSALM 32:6–11 NIV

- Time is limited, and seeking God is presented as an urgent matter to do while it's still possible. What does that urgency mean for you today?

- What do the "rising mighty waters" described in today's passage symbolize for you? What could God's protection from these waters be in particular?

- Where do you feel most safe and secure? How can that idea help you relate to the safety and security you feel with God?

- How can you help your children learn to rely on God and to be open to God's instruction in their lives?

- Recall a time you resisted God's instruction. How can you remain open to God's instruction and counsel?

- Consider how you have tried to influence people and help them make better decisions. What does this passage share about God's preferred way to influence you?

- When you imagine God's gaze toward you, how would you describe it? Consider for a moment that God's gaze is described as "loving" and what that means.

- Looking over the past week, where were you placing your trust? Who were you learning from? How can you respond to the invitation in today's passage?

- When you receive the assurance of God's unfailing love, you will have an opportunity to rejoice. How can rejoicing become a more regular practice for you and your family?

Lord, I trust in Your unfailing mercy and Your loving gaze as I learn to trust in You throughout my day. May I find safety and security in You, and may I remain open to learning from You and following in the direction that You set for my life. Help me to influence my children with love and kindness so that they will make good decisions and remain faithful to You. Amen.

TAKE COURAGE—
JESUS IS HERE

Immediately after this, Jesus insisted that his disciples get back into the boat and cross to the other side of the lake, while he sent the people home. After sending them home, he went up into the hills by himself to pray. Night fell while he was there alone. Meanwhile, the disciples were in trouble far away from land, for a strong wind had risen, and they were fighting heavy waves. About three o'clock in the morning Jesus came toward them, walking on the water. When the disciples saw him walking on the water, they were terrified. In their fear, they cried out, "It's a ghost!" But Jesus spoke to them at once. "Don't be afraid," he said. "Take courage. I am here!"

MATTHEW 14:22–27 NLT

* After performing a miracle, Jesus made sure everyone was sent on their way, and then He took time to pray alone before God. When do you need some time in solitude for prayer?

* How can you make prayer a priority when you serve others or get involved in ministry? In what ways could you benefit from a time of solitude after serving others?

* Are there times when you have been struggling and found that God has unexpectedly been present? What does the reaction of Jesus' disciples show you in this story?

- How does the presence of Jesus offer comfort to you in tumultuous situations? Are there ways that you can become more aware of Jesus when your life becomes chaotic?

- What kind of peace does Jesus offer when you're caught in a storm? How does Jesus help you in times of trial and uncertainty?

- Why do you think Jesus chose to walk on the water rather than simply calming the storm? What do you think He was revealing to them? What is He revealing to you?

- What were the disciples expecting from God when they were caught in the storm? What does their reaction tell you?

Jesus, I trust that You remain with me when I am trapped in storms and that You can bring courage and peace when everything else in my life appears out of sorts. May I look on Your power and Your promises, remembering that You are faithful to stand by Your people. Guide me to the paths that lead to peace so that I may testify of Your love to others. Amen.

WORSHIP THE LORD WITH ALL YOUR HEART

"Don't be afraid," Samuel reassured them. "You have certainly done wrong, but make sure now that you worship the LORD with all your heart, and don't turn your back on him. Don't go back to worshiping worthless idols that cannot help or rescue you—they are totally useless! The LORD will not abandon his people, because that would dishonor his great name. For it has pleased the LORD to make you his very own people. As for me, I will certainly not sin against the LORD by ending my prayers for you. And I will continue to teach you what is good and right. But be sure to fear the LORD and faithfully serve him. Think of all the wonderful things he has done for you. But if you continue to sin, you and your king will be swept away."

1 SAMUEL 12:20-25 NLT

- What did the people of Israel have to fear as they looked forward to their future under their king? Had their actions contributed to the fear they now faced? How have you managed your own fears?

- Past failures and sins didn't spell the end of the people of Israel. Samuel encouraged them to continue to pursue God with all their heart. Is there something you can confess or surrender to God as you pray today?

- Have you struggled to hope or to believe in God's love and mercy for you? How can you reach out in faith to God?

- Why were idols such a persistent problem for the people of Israel? What did idols promise to do that they couldn't trust God to do? Was there something different about idols that made them more appealing? Do you struggle with trusting in things other than God to solve your problems?

- Samuel believed his calling was to continually pray for the people of Israel to the point that it would be a sin to stop praying for his people. Do you have a burden to pray for someone or for an outcome? How can you pursue that burden to pray today?

Lord, You want me to fully rely on You and to leave the false hopes of idols behind. May I listen for Your direction and offer prayers for others so that they will know You and the power of Your Name in their lives. May I remain committed to Your calling for my life so that I faithfully complete all that You have asked me to do and not stray from what You have taught me. Amen.

PRAYER AND EXAMINATION GO TOGETHER

Test yourselves to see if you are in the faith; examine yourselves! Or do you not recognize this about yourselves, that Jesus Christ is in you—unless indeed you fail the test? But I trust that you will realize that we ourselves do not fail the test. Now we pray to God that you do no wrong; not that we ourselves may appear approved, but that you may do what is right, even though we may appear unapproved. For we can do nothing against the truth, but only for the truth. For we rejoice when we ourselves are weak but you are strong; this we also pray for, that you be made complete. For this reason I am writing these things while absent, so that when present I need not use severity, in accordance with the authority which the Lord gave me for building up and not for tearing down.

2 Corinthians 13:5–10 nasb

- There is a very real danger of neglecting the gift of Christ's presence in your life. If you have accepted Christ as your Lord, what would it look like to examine yourself today to ensure that you are in the faith?

- Obedience to the commands of Christ is repeatedly mentioned as a sign of one's authentic faith. Are you struggling in a particular area of your life today? How can you confess your need for healing and transformation? Why is this confession important?

- Are there times that you have forgotten about the presence of Christ in your life? How would remembering this change the way you approach today?

- Paul saw himself as a parent who was giving freely of himself for the benefit of his children in the church. How have you made sacrifices for the sake of others? Are there ways that God may be calling you to serve in your church or community?

- Authority wasn't a hammer that Paul used carelessly. He far preferred to use his authority to build up others. What kind of authority and influence do you have? How can you use your authority and influence well for the encouragement of your fellow believers?

Jesus, examine my heart, and reveal if there is anything I have held back or if I must address any wrong. May I live my life according to Your commands and with a sensitivity to the Spirit's leading so that I remain in line with Your will and invest time and energy in serving Your people. Amen.

DO YOU BELIEVE GOD HEARS YOUR PRAYERS?

And when the time for the burning of incense came, all the assembled worshipers were praying outside. Then an angel of the Lord appeared to him, standing at the right side of the altar of incense. When Zechariah saw him, he was startled and was gripped with fear. But the angel said to him: "Do not be afraid, Zechariah; your prayer has been heard. Your wife Elizabeth will bear you a son, and you are to call him John. He will be a joy and delight to you, and many will rejoice because of his birth, for he will be great in the sight of the Lord. He is never to take wine or other fermented drink, and he will be filled with the Holy Spirit even before he is born. He will bring back many of the people of Israel to the Lord their God."

LUKE 1:10–16 NIV

♦ Zechariah had been praying for a child for so long that he could hardly believe an angel's message about the coming birth of John. How have you felt when a longtime prayer hasn't been answered?

♦ Zechariah immediately doubted the angel's message, which may be surprising since the presence of the angel was a good reason to believe. However, unbelief can be strong, even in the presence of an angel. In what ways have you struggled with unbelief?

♦ God had a plan for John right from the moment of his conception, filling him with the Holy Spirit. What is the significance of being filled with the Holy Spirit for ministry? How has the Holy Spirit prepared you to serve others?

• God planned to use John as a special prophet to bring the people of Israel back to God. Even when Israel had been unfaithful to the Lord's commands throughout history, God still reached out to His people with mercy and compassion. What message do you see in John's ministry?

Lord, I trust that You hear my prayers and that You will give a response at the appropriate time. I trust You with the timing and details of my prayer requests, knowing that You will act within my best interests and the best interests of others. May I see You act on my behalf, and may I bless many others through the work You begin in me. Amen.

GOD KNOWS WHAT YOU NEED

"When you pray, don't babble on and on as the Gentiles do. They think their prayers are answered merely by repeating their words again and again. Don't be like them, for your Father knows exactly what you need even before you ask him! Pray like this: Our Father in heaven, may your name be kept holy. May your Kingdom come soon. May your will be done on earth, as it is in heaven. Give us today the food we need, and forgive us our sins, as we have forgiven those who sin against us. And don't let us yield to temptation, but rescue us from the evil one."

Matthew 6:7–13 NLT

- What do you think you need to do in order for God to hear your prayers?

- What is the contrast between how the Gentiles at the time of Jesus prayed and how Jesus wants His disciples to pray?

- When could repeating a familiar prayer or passage of scripture be helpful for you? When could that kind of repetition undermine your prayers?

- What is the significance of Jesus encouraging you to call God your "Father" when you pray?

- Consider how a father remains aware of the needs of his children. How does that shape the way you pray to God your Father?

- If God already knows what you need before you even ask, why is it important to still pray and ask God for help?

- Why does this prayer Jesus taught His disciples start with an awareness of God's holiness and a petition for God's Kingdom to come soon?

- What does it look like when your own will is being done rather than God's will?

- Why might Jesus address God's will first before making a petition for God's provision?

- What is the significance of forgiving others while also seeking forgiveness from God?

- If Jesus is aware of the dangers of temptation and the schemes of the evil one, how could those threats change the way you pray?

- How can this prayer from Jesus help you teach your children to pray?

Father, thank You for the words that Jesus gave us to pray and for the assurance that You are aware of and concerned about my needs. May Your will and Your Kingdom work come first in my life as I find contentment and peace in continuing the ministry that Jesus began. May I pray with peace and confidence in Your loving care, and may my children learn to trust You in their own quiet moments of prayer and in their times of great need. Amen.

A TIME FOR PRAYER AND FASTING

Jesus responded, "Do wedding guests fast while celebrating with the groom? Of course not. But someday the groom will be taken away from them, and then they will fast." Then Jesus gave them this illustration: "No one tears a piece of cloth from a new garment and uses it to patch an old garment. For then the new garment would be ruined, and the new patch wouldn't even match the old garment. And no one puts new wine into old wineskins. For the new wine would burst the wineskins, spilling the wine and ruining the skins. New wine must be stored in new wineskins. But no one who drinks the old wine seems to want the new wine. 'The old is just fine,' they say."

LUKE 5:34-39 NLT

+ Jesus brought a time of celebration and joy, as He announced the time of God's favor and made a point of feasting and celebrating. However, those who wait for His return are in a season of fasting. Which practices can help you prepare for God and wait patiently?

+ How did fasting draw attention away from Jesus during His ministry? What can you learn from Jesus' teaching about religious practices when He noted that His followers would not fast while He was with them?

+ Just as new wine needs a new container, the teachings of Jesus required a new way of viewing

God's commandments and an understanding of when to celebrate and when to mourn. Is God calling you into a time of repentance, anticipation, or celebration?

* How have you seen God move you from one season to another over the years? What prepared you to receive the new things God was doing in your life?

* Why is it hard for religious people to leave a familiar practice or belief behind? How has Jesus challenged you to trust in Him rather than in what you are familiar with?

Jesus, open my eyes to the ways I overlook Your presence and direction when I become too focused on what's familiar and comfortable in my life. Help me to receive Your direction and wisdom so that I can wisely step forward in line with Your dreams and desires. May I recognize the seasons for fasting and discernment, as well as the seasons for celebration and gratitude, receiving the gifts You gladly give to Your people. Amen.

AN EXAMPLE OF PERFECT UNITY

Jesus said to them, "Very truly, I tell you, the Son can do nothing on his own, but only what he sees the Father doing; for whatever the Father does, the Son does likewise. The Father loves the Son and shows him all that he himself is doing; and he will show him greater works than these, so that you will be astonished. Indeed, just as the Father raises the dead and gives them life, so also the Son gives life to whomever he wishes. The Father judges no one but has given all judgment to the Son, so that all may honor the Son just as they honor the Father. Anyone who does not honor the Son does not honor the Father who sent him."

JOHN 5:19–23 NRSV

- Jesus speaks about His actions being united fully with the Father and what He sees the Father doing. What is the significance of this unity of purpose and action within the Trinity?

- Why would Jesus compare Himself to a son and God the Father to a father? What from your own father/child relationships helps you understand this nature of God?

- When you imagine what God is like, how does it compare to the type of God that Jesus describes in His relationship with God the Father?

- How can this unity of Father and Son in the Trinity help you imagine the possibilities of unity with your children?

- Why is it important for the Father to show the Son all of the works that He is doing?

- Consider where you've lost hope or what you fear the most in the future. How can the words of Jesus in this passage offer you assurance and peace?

- What does it mean that the Son "gives life to whomever he wishes"? What is the nature of this life, and when do you think you can enjoy its benefits?

- Jesus often said that He did not come into the world in order to judge it. What does this approach to judgment mean to you in your relationship with God? What does this absence of judgment in the present moment mean for your relationship with other people?

- The Ten Commandments speak of honoring your mother and father, and Jesus expects people to honor Him and the Father. What does it look like to honor God and to honor another person?

Father, thank You for the new life and unity that You brought through Jesus, Your Son. May I live with Him and with You in unity of purpose and Spirit so that I can do what You desire and share Your message freely with others. May my family enjoy the life and freedom that You bring through their unity with You. Amen.

LEARNING TO DELIGHT IN GOD'S COMMANDS

Let your steadfast love come to me, O LORD, your salvation according to your promise. Then I shall have an answer for those who taunt me, for I trust in your word. Do not take the word of truth utterly out of my mouth, for my hope is in your ordinances. I will keep your law continually, forever and ever. I shall walk at liberty, for I have sought your precepts. I will also speak of your decrees before kings, and shall not be put to shame; I find my delight in your commandments, because I love them. I revere your commandments, which I love, and I will meditate on your statutes. Remember your word to your servant, in which you have made me hope. This is my comfort in my distress, that your promise gives me life.

PSALM 119:41-50 NRSV

- Where are you today in relation to God's steadfast love? Are you aware of it, doubting it, or unsure that it truly applies to you? How can you ask God for His love to become more present in your life?

- How have you responded to those who have taunted you or called God into question?

- Are there commands or teachings from scripture that you have found particularly comforting or hopeful? What does it look like to find your hope in God's ordinances today?

- The freedom that comes in Christ comes in part by learning to view obedience as freedom compared to past slavery to sin. How have you found freedom by walking in God's precepts? Why is this sometimes counterintuitive?

- By keeping God's laws and delighting in the freedom they bring, God's people will be more naturally disposed to share them with others. How have you seen the truth of scripture become easier to share with others as you make time for it?

- Where do you tend to seek comfort in times of distress? How can you take greater comfort in God's promises and teachings?

Lord, I turn to Your promises and commandments today as the source of my delight and my hope for the future. I trust that Your Word is reliable and certain as the foundation of my life so that I can speak to others with confidence and remain unmoved when conflict arises or others mock my dependence on You. May I enjoy the liberty of Your law and freely share its hope with others. Amen.

JESUS IS WILLING TO HELP

While He was in one of the cities, behold, there was a man covered with leprosy; and when he saw Jesus, he fell on his face and implored Him, saying, "Lord, if You are willing, You can make me clean." And He stretched out His hand and touched him, saying, "I am willing; be cleansed." And immediately the leprosy left him. And He ordered him to tell no one, "But go and show yourself to the priest and make an offering for your cleansing, just as Moses commanded, as a testimony to them." But the news about Him was spreading even farther, and large crowds were gathering to hear Him and to be healed of their sicknesses. But Jesus Himself would often slip away to the wilderness and pray.

LUKE 5:12–16 NASB

- ◆ The desperation of this man comes through in his plea to Jesus, expecting that Jesus would reject him like so many others had due to his disease. How have you experienced rejection in your life? Does that shape how you imagine God sees you?

- ◆ It's interesting to note that the man didn't doubt the power of Jesus, but he did doubt whether Jesus valued him enough to take a moment to heal him. Do you find yourself doubting the power of Jesus or the willingness of Jesus? Why?

- ◆ Why did Jesus instruct the leper to show himself to the priest? How have you seen others respond to the times when God brings blessing or healing into your life?

- Jesus instructed the man to tell no one but the priest, whereas we can imagine someone today wanting a healing to be widely publicized. What is the value of keeping a spiritual experience to yourself? How do you balance the value of a testimony with the secret work that God is doing in your life?

- What do you think Jesus gained by often removing Himself from the crowds so that He could pray in solitude? How does time away from people nurture your own spiritual growth and ability to minister to others?

Jesus, You are present, willing, and able to bring Your healing into my life. I trust Your power and concern for me because I am Your beloved child and Your Spirit rests in my life. May I take my concerns and problems to You, surrendering them to Your care and trusting that You will address them at the right time. May I find the solitude I need today to remain aware of Your present love and power. Amen.

DEVOTION TO GOD IS COURAGEOUS

But when Daniel learned that the law had been signed, he went home and knelt down as usual in his upstairs room, with its windows open toward Jerusalem. He prayed three times a day, just as he had always done, giving thanks to his God. Then the officials went together to Daniel's house and found him praying and asking for God's help. So they went straight to the king and reminded him about his law. "Did you not sign a law that for the next thirty days any person who prays to anyone, divine or human—except to you, Your Majesty—will be thrown into the den of lions?" "Yes," the king replied, "that decision stands; it is an official law of the Medes and Persians that cannot be revoked." Then they told the king, "That man Daniel, one of the captives from Judah, is ignoring you and your law. He still prays to his God three times a day."

DANIEL 6:10–13 NLT

- Do you have a typical prayer practice or location that you turn to each day? Considering Daniel's steadfast practice, how could a regular time and location for prayer help you?

- Without a regular time to pray, what have you seen happen in your life when adversity strikes or your schedule becomes busy?

- While Daniel faced severe consequences *because of* his prayers to the Lord, have you found that there are consequences for *neglecting* prayer? What do you think prompted Daniel to continue praying even when his life was in danger?

• Knowing that some Christians in the world face isolation, persecution, or even violence for their faithfulness to God, how can you pray today for their safety and encouragement? Do you have a particular connection to a nation where Christians face limitations or persecution?

• Political agendas can exploit religious devotion in order to accomplish nefarious goals. How can you remain vigilant for the ways that politicians manipulate people of faith for their own ends?

Lord, You have remained faithful and compassionate to Your people throughout history, standing by all who remain committed to You. May I find the time and space each day to pray to You, entrusting my worries into Your care and giving thanks for the many blessings You have given me. Give me courage to face those who oppose my devotion to You, and may Your deliverance in my life become a testimony to others. Amen.

PRAY FOR THE PEACE
OF YOUR CITY

I was glad when they said to me, "Let us go to the house of the LORD!" Our feet are standing within your gates, O Jerusalem. Jerusalem—built as a city that is bound firmly together. To it the tribes go up, the tribes of the LORD, as was decreed for Israel, to give thanks to the name of the LORD. For there the thrones for judgment were set up, the thrones of the house of David. Pray for the peace of Jerusalem: "May they prosper who love you. Peace be within your walls, and security within your towers." For the sake of my relatives and friends I will say, "Peace be within you." For the sake of the house of the LORD our God, I will seek your good.

PSALM 122:1–9 NRSV

- The people of Israel viewed Jerusalem as a joyful place to go to worship God. Where do you find peace and joy in your worship?

- Why did the Lord decree that the people of Israel gather together for worship three times each year? How do regular worship assemblies help you grow in your faith? What are the other benefits of gathering together in larger groups?

- What are the reasons some people avoid church or feel alienated from the Church? How can you help those who feel unable to join a church at this time? How can you make your church more welcoming to visitors in general?

- Why is it helpful to give thanks to God as part of a group?

- Peace and political stability make it possible for God's people to worship freely without the fear of war or displacement. How can you pray for peace today?

- Praying for peace takes the focus of prayer away from just your own safety and well-being. It extends your awareness to the needs of your family, your city, and even your enemies, praying that there will be peace for all concerned. Who is most in need of prayers for peace today?

Jesus, You are the Prince of Peace who brings reconciliation to God and humanity, saving us from our selfish attachments and unrestrained greed as we find contentment and joy in You. I will give thanks for Your mercies that are new every morning and the gift of community and the support it brings. May my city and nation find peace and security today, and grant me the freedom to worship You without the dark clouds of war looming. Amen.

APPROACH GOD
WITH CONFESSION

*To some who were confident of their own
righteousness and looked down on everyone else,
Jesus told this parable: "Two men went up to the
temple to pray, one a Pharisee and the other a
tax collector. The Pharisee stood by himself and
prayed: 'God, I thank you that I am not like other
people—robbers, evildoers, adulterers—or even
like this tax collector. I fast twice a week and give
a tenth of all I get.' But the tax collector stood at
a distance. He would not even look up to heaven,
but beat his breast and said, 'God, have mercy on
me, a sinner.' I tell you that this man, rather than
the other, went home justified before God. For all
those who exalt themselves will be humbled, and
those who humble themselves will be exalted."*

LUKE 18:9-14 NIV

- Why did the two men approach God in prayer? What were they hoping to get out of prayer? Take some time to examine your motives in prayer. What do you expect will happen?

- There are two approaches to justifying yourself in this passage. One man focused on what he had done, and the other relied on God's forgiveness. How can you rely on God to justify you today?

- How does comparison become a trap for the Pharisee in this passage? How have you seen comparison become a distraction in your life?

- Christians have prayed the tax collector's prayer for centuries to remain focused on God and to fight off temptation. How can a regular reminder of God's mercy for your sin help you pray more often and with more confidence?

- The tax collector was praying in public, but he stood far off and showed remorse for his sins rather than trying to convince others that he was righteous. How have you expressed sorrow in your own life? When is it appropriate to express sorrow publicly?

- When have you humbled yourself before God? How have you seen God work in your life when you are humble and place yourself at God's mercy?

Jesus, I confess that I have fallen short of Your commandments and have chosen my own way. Although I have sinned, I trust in Your great mercy for sinners and I look to You for restoration. Guard my heart from the sins of pride and comparison, as I cannot justify myself or exalt myself at the expense of others. May I become a herald of Your mercy to others. Amen.

RETURN TO GOD'S BLESSINGS

*In those days the house of Judah will walk with the
house of Israel, and they will come together from
the land of the north to the land that I gave your
fathers as an inheritance. "Then I said, 'How I would
set you among My sons and give you a pleasant
land, the most beautiful inheritance of the nations!'
And I said, 'You shall call Me, My Father, and not
turn away from following Me.' Surely, as a woman
treacherously departs from her lover, so you have
dealt treacherously with Me, O house of Israel,"
declares the LORD. A voice is heard on the bare
heights, the weeping, and the supplications of the
sons of Israel; because they have perverted their way,
they have forgotten the LORD their God. "Return, O
faithless sons, I will heal your faithlessness." "Behold,
we come to You; for You are the LORD our God."*

JEREMIAH 3:18-22 NASB

- When you have disobeyed God's commands, what
  did you hope to gain from your actions?

- God promised to treat Israel like His sons, giving
  the people a pleasant land and inheritance. Why did
  the people of Israel turn away from God if these
  were promised to them?

- How did God describe the disobedience of the
  Israelites when they neglected God's inheritance?
  What does that mean for your choices about obeying
  God?

- What is the appropriate response to disobedience and forgetting about God?

- How have you felt when you've made poor choices? What do you imagine God's response will be when you repent? How does this passage describe God's response?

- When your children disobey, how have you felt about them? What would you expect them to do to make things right?

- How does this passage model some examples of parents and children seeking reconciliation with one another?

- Disobedience is a big deal, but God promises to heal His faithless children. How do you communicate both the gravity of sin and the mercy and grace of God to your children?

Father, I have failed to listen to Your commands and have resisted returning to You when it's clearly for my own good. Help me to see my failures with clarity, the seriousness of my sin with honesty, and the presence of Your mercy and healing with faith. May I help my children learn to obey You and to return to You for their healing when they fail, so that they can live in the peace and blessing of God's chosen children. Amen.

THE LORD IS WORTHY OF PRAISE

Praise the LORD! Praise the name of the LORD; give praise, O servants of the LORD, you that stand in the house of the LORD, in the courts of the house of our God. Praise the LORD, for the LORD is good; sing to his name, for he is gracious. For the LORD has chosen Jacob for himself, Israel as his own possession. For I know that the LORD is great; our Lord is above all gods. Whatever the LORD pleases he does, in heaven and on earth, in the seas and all deeps. He it is who makes the clouds rise at the end of the earth; he makes lightnings for the rain and brings out the wind from his storehouses.

PSALM 135:1-7 NRSV

- Who have you praised recently? What did you praise in this person? How is praise a part of your worship of God? Do you find that praise comes naturally, or do you struggle to think of something to mention? Why?

- How have you experienced God's goodness and graciousness? How would your life be different if God's goodness and graciousness had not come to you?

- What does it mean that God has chosen you to be among His people? When you feel alienated from God, how can you take comfort and security in this knowledge?

- If you spent time comparing God to every other power, authority, and leader in this world, how would

God stack up? When have you struggled to believe that God is greater than any other power or authority on earth?

- Take a moment to meditate on the power of God over His creation. How does reflecting on God's power impact your perspective for today?

- How does reflecting on God's control of the elements and power over creation impact what you believe about God's power in your life?

Lord, I will meditate on Your power over creation and the mercy You have shown by adopting me into Your family. I will stand among Your people and sing Your praises with thankfulness and hope. May I find Your favor today as I put my trust in You and wait for Your deliverance from every fear, every power, and every discouragement in this world. Just as Your people trusted You to bring rain for their crops, I will trust that You can free me from the things that threaten my prosperity and future. Amen.

HOW TO STAND FIRM IN PRAYER

Stand firm therefore, HAVING GIRDED YOUR LOINS WITH TRUTH, and HAVING PUT ON THE BREASTPLATE OF RIGHTEOUSNESS, and having shod YOUR FEET WITH THE PREPARATION OF THE GOSPEL OF PEACE; in addition to all, taking up the shield of faith with which you will be able to extinguish all the flaming arrows of the evil one. And take THE HELMET OF SALVATION, and the sword of the Spirit, which is the word of God. With all prayer and petition pray at all times in the Spirit, and with this in view, be on the alert with all perseverance and petition for all the saints, and pray on my behalf, that utterance may be given to me in the opening of my mouth, to make known with boldness the mystery of the gospel.

EPHESIANS 6:14-19 NASB

- ◆ How does the truth help you stand firm and be prepared for the challenges of life? When did confusion or error undermine your ability to stand?

- ◆ When have you experienced opposition or conflict from the evil one? How has faith helped you fend off these attacks to your confidence in God?

- ◆ What kinds of prayer could you use as you "pray at all times"? Paul mentioned petitions, but how could laments, praise, thanksgiving, intercession, or silent prayer help you pray more regularly and effectively?

- What does it mean to pray "in the Spirit"? How has the Spirit helped you pray? Is it possible that you weren't aware of the Spirit's prayers at work in you? How does this speak to the way you pray today?

- Why is it urgent for you to be on the alert, praying at all times and making petitions for the saints?

- How did Paul see prayer impacting the way he shared the Gospel? Is sharing the Gospel challenging or easy for you? How can you make sharing the Gospel part of your prayers today?

Jesus, help me to stand firm in the truth granted through the Spirit's insight, and may my prayers enjoy the benefit of the Spirit's advocacy and direction. I ask for the security of faith and the protection of the Spirit as I seek Your will and confidently share the message of Your salvation with others. May I remain mindful of the needs of others so that my prayers are continually lifting them to Your care. Amen.

WE ARE GOD'S CHILDREN

See how very much our Father loves us, for he calls us his children, and that is what we are! But the people who belong to this world don't recognize that we are God's children because they don't know him. Dear friends, we are already God's children, but he has not yet shown us what we will be like when Christ appears. But we do know that we will be like him, for we will see him as he really is. And all who have this eager expectation will keep themselves pure, just as he is pure.

1 JOHN 3:1-3 NLT

- ◆ What is your reaction to John writing that God is a Father who loves you? What can prevent you from seeing yourself as God's beloved child?

- ◆ If you are indeed God's child, then what does that mean for you today? How does that impact your mindset and the choices you make today?

- ◆ This passage addresses God's unseen promises that will one day be fulfilled. Why is the relationship of a father and his children helpful when considering the unseen hope you have in Christ?

- ◆ John is concerned with identity in this passage, especially who you belong to. Why would John mention that those who belong to the world will see you differently than you are in God?

- ◆ Besides the people of the world not recognizing God's goodness in you, it's also likely that you haven't seen what God's goodness means for you. Why is it so hard to wait for God's likeness to show up in your life?

- What kind of hope and assurance does Jesus offer you today? What do you have to do to make sure you experience that hope?

- Waiting for good things is a hard part of childhood. How does your experience as a parent help you understand this passage?

- How does John expect his readers to live now that they know about the hope that Jesus promises for them?

Father, thank You for calling me Your child and for giving me the hope that I will one day be changed into Your likeness and will experience the complete hope that You have promised through Your servant John. Help me to look beyond what others see and my own limitations so that I can place my hope in Your future holiness and glory. May my family experience the security of knowing that we are Your beloved children who can wait patiently for the complete revelation of our place in You. Amen.

GOD HELPS OUR UNBELIEF WHEN WE DOUBT

"What do you mean, 'If I can'?" Jesus asked. "Anything is possible if a person believes." The father instantly cried out, "I do believe, but help me overcome my unbelief!" When Jesus saw that the crowd of onlookers was growing, he rebuked the evil spirit. "Listen, you spirit that makes this boy unable to hear and speak," he said. "I command you to come out of this child and never enter him again!" Then the spirit screamed and threw the boy into another violent convulsion and left him. The boy appeared to be dead. A murmur ran through the crowd as people said, "He's dead." But Jesus took him by the hand and helped him to his feet, and he stood up. Afterward, when Jesus was alone in the house with his disciples, they asked him, "Why couldn't we cast out that evil spirit?" Jesus replied, "This kind can be cast out only by prayer."

MARK 9:23-29 NLT

- When have you felt that it's necessary to hedge on your prayers, offering God an out? How does today's scripture suggest we can respond to the temptation of doubt?

- While anything is possible for a person who believes, not every prayer request is answered as expected. How do you reconcile the tension between the call to believe and the reality that many face with prayer requests?

- The disciples had tried to cast out a demon, but they failed. What do you think Jesus did differently by praying for the boy? How can you adapt prayer for the different spiritual challenges you face?

- Imagining yourself in this father's place, are there times when you have confused the failures of Christians with the failures of God? How did Jesus lead him out of his error?

- When you've had a bewildering or confusing spiritual experience, how did you handle your questions? Who do you ask for guidance or help? How do you think Jesus' disciples changed their prayers in response to Jesus?

Jesus, You encourage me to live in obedience and to trust You so that I can pray with confidence and freedom from worry. Help me to bring my cares and burdens to You so that I can experience Your provision and encourage others to place their hope in You. May I pray with persistence and commitment for those in need, holding on to the hope that You hear my prayers and will surely respond. Amen.

YOU ARE KNOWN
AND LOVED BY GOD

O LORD, you have searched me and known me. You know when I sit down and when I rise up; you discern my thoughts from far away. You search out my path and my lying down, and are acquainted with all my ways. Even before a word is on my tongue, O LORD, you know it completely. You hem me in, behind and before, and lay your hand upon me. Such knowledge is too wonderful for me; it is so high that I cannot attain it. Where can I go from your spirit? Or where can I flee from your presence? If I ascend to heaven, you are there; if I make my bed in Sheol, you are there. If I take the wings of the morning and settle at the farthest limits of the sea, even there your hand shall lead me, and your right hand shall hold me fast.

PSALM 139:1-10 NRSV

* When have you been tempted to run away from God or to resist the presence of God? What does it mean to you that you cannot flee from God's love and presence?

* Do you find it comforting or disconcerting to know that God is intimately aware of your thoughts and daily actions? How would it impact your prayers if you trusted that God is fully aware of your thoughts and still actively seeks you out?

* In what kinds of situations have you asked God for guidance or help? How have you learned to rely on God's presence when the path forward is uncertain?

- When have you made a poor choice or taken a detour in life? What if you believed that God remained with you during that time, calling you back to Himself and accepting you as you recognized your wrongs?

- If God is so completely present for you, what may be preventing you from experiencing God's loving presence at times?

Father, You are present with me today as You have always been, whether I have been close or far away from You. Guide me back to Your side, teach me to speak with grace and mercy, and instruct me in Your ways so that I can fully enjoy the abundance of You. May I continually experience the wonder and the joy of You, rejoicing in the gift of Your Spirit as You lead me each day. Amen.

HOW GOD BUILDS UP HIS PEOPLE

By the grace God has given me, I laid a foundation as a wise builder, and someone else is building on it. But each one should build with care. For no one can lay any foundation other than the one already laid, which is Jesus Christ. If anyone builds on this foundation using gold, silver, costly stones, wood, hay or straw, their work will be shown for what it is, because the Day will bring it to light. It will be revealed with fire, and the fire will test the quality of each person's work. If what has been built survives, the builder will receive a reward. If it is burned up, the builder will suffer loss but yet will be saved—even though only as one escaping through the flames. Don't you know that you yourselves are God's temple and that God's Spirit dwells in your midst?

1 CORINTHIANS 3:10-16 NIV

♦ Paul partnered with others to grow the Church. In what roles have you seen God use you to build up others?

♦ What do you think Paul referred to when he talked about building a foundation? What would you describe as foundational in your life?

♦ What does it look like for Christ to be the foundation of your life? How does Christ provide a strong foundation that will last?

- When you consider the other kinds of things that could provide a foundation in life, what would you list for yourself? In what ways can these things fail you?

- While Paul did not say Christians will lose their salvation when God tests their works, he did note that anything built on a foundation other than Christ will be burned up. How does that speak to you? Do you have anxiety about judgment? How can you pray about the foundation of your life today?

- What does it mean for you to be God's temple for the Holy Spirit? What difference does the presence of God's Spirit make in your life? Are there ways that you would like to see the Spirit become more prominent in your life?

Jesus, I trust that You are the foundation of my life and that relying on You will help me honor You and love others. Save me from the fruitless works and false foundations that will pass away, and guide me toward the hope and confidence that You give. May I learn to rest in Your present Spirit today. Amen.

GOD WILL CHANGE YOUR HEART

"I will show how holy my great name is—the name on which you brought shame among the nations. And when I reveal my holiness through you before their very eyes, says the Sovereign LORD, then the nations will know that I am the LORD. For I will gather you up from all the nations and bring you home again to your land. Then I will sprinkle clean water on you, and you will be clean. Your filth will be washed away, and you will no longer worship idols. And I will give you a new heart, and I will put a new spirit in you. I will take out your stony, stubborn heart and give you a tender, responsive heart. And I will put my Spirit in you so that you will follow my decrees and be careful to obey my regulations."

Ezekiel 36:23–27 NLT

- If you are seeking to repent of sin and to be restored by God today, consider asking God to help restore your heart and your spirit. How does God's work in your heart and spirit impact your actions?

- While God had called His people to repent and to change their ways for generations, they struggled to follow through. Is there an area of your life where you especially struggle to obey? How can you depend on God as you pray about it?

- How did the revelation of God's holiness and greatness impact His people? When have you experienced the goodness and holiness of God?

- When God revealed Himself to His people, He expected the nations to witness His glory too. How can God's transforming power in your life also impact others?

- Would you describe your heart as stubborn? What would a responsive or tender heart look like? How does God expect His people to be transformed?

- Are there times when you have felt distant from God? How did you begin to reach out to God again?

Father, You long to soften my heart and to make me receptive and responsive to Your message. I depend on You and Your indwelling Spirit to help me pay attention to Your commands and to live in holiness and purity. Turn my heart away from the idols that capture my attention and loyalty, so that I learn to depend on You alone. May my life serve as a testimony to the ways You can transform lives and bring renewal. Amen.

FAITHFULNESS IS COSTLY
BUT REWARDED

*Jesus went out, along with His disciples, to the villages
of Caesarea Philippi; and on the way He questioned
His disciples, saying to them, "Who do people say that
I am?" . . . And He continued by questioning them, "But
who do you say that I am?" Peter answered and said
to Him, "You are the Christ." And He warned them to
tell no one about Him. And He began to teach them
that the Son of Man must suffer many things and
be rejected by the elders and the chief priests and
the scribes, and be killed, and after three days rise
again. And He was stating the matter plainly. And
Peter took Him aside and began to rebuke Him. But
turning around and seeing His disciples, He rebuked
Peter and said, "Get behind Me, Satan; for you are
not setting your mind on God's interests, but man's."*

MARK 8:27, 29-33 NASB

+ Why did Jesus ask His disciples for their thoughts on
  His identity? How would you reply to Jesus if asked
  that same question today?

+ What is the significance of your answer to Jesus'
  question? How does your answer determine the way
  you pray, let alone how often you pray?

+ Jesus explained to His disciples that following God
  would be costly for Him and then invited them to do
  the same—taking up figurative crosses after He took
  up His literal cross. How did the disciples respond to

this challenging message? What is at stake for you as you read this passage?

- When you consider all that Jesus gave up in order to do God's will, what do you think God is asking you to sacrifice today to follow Him?

- Are there ways that you can relate to Peter's rebukes? What had influenced Peter's thinking about the fate of Jesus? What kinds of influences have impacted your decisions and leaps of faith?

- Jesus went on to describe His generation as adulterous and sinful. What do you think prompted Him to use those terms? How would you describe your generation?

Jesus, I am in need of Your wisdom and guidance for my life so that my own desires and plans will not drown out Your costly call to discipleship. May I trust in Your love and the wisdom of Your indwelling Spirit so that I can discern what Your will is and then act with courage to go where You have called me. Amen.

TAKE TIME TO MEDITATE ON GOD'S WORKS

Great is the L<small>ORD</small>, and greatly to be praised; his greatness is unsearchable. One generation shall laud your works to another, and shall declare your mighty acts. On the glorious splendor of your majesty, and on your wondrous works, I will meditate. The might of your awesome deeds shall be proclaimed, and I will declare your greatness. They shall celebrate the fame of your abundant goodness, and shall sing aloud of your righteousness. The L<small>ORD</small> is gracious and merciful, slow to anger and abounding in steadfast love. The L<small>ORD</small> is good to all, and his compassion is over all that he has made. All your works shall give thanks to you, O L<small>ORD</small>, and all your faithful shall bless you.

P<small>SALM</small> 145:3–10 <small>NRSV</small>

- What has been on your mind today? How can you grow in awareness of God's presence throughout your day? Is there something in particular that gets in the way of your awareness of God?

- In this psalm, there is a strong emphasis on celebrating God's works, declaring God's greatness, and proclaiming God's goodness and righteousness. What would you sing about or praise if you were writing your own psalm to celebrate God? Are there ways you would like to experience God to praise Him more regularly?

- How has God acted on your behalf? Are you hesitant to share about the works of God in your life? What has held you back from witnessing to others about the ways you have experienced God?

- When you consider the anger of God, do you imagine God being fast or slow to grow angry? What does it mean for you that God is slow to anger?

- Are you more likely to imagine God as angry or loving? How does this psalm express those emotions in God?

- This psalm describes God as gracious, merciful, and compassionate. Take time to meditate on these qualities in God. How does this impact the way you view God?

Lord, You have shown Yourself as gracious and compassionate to past generations. May I experience Your goodness and see Your faithfulness with my own eyes so that I can celebrate Your works with gladness. I ask that future generations will continue to learn of Your goodness and that they will be prompted to seek You in prayer because of Your graciousness, mercy, and compassion for Your people. Amen.

TOPICAL INDEX